To Ann & Glenn

Read and enjoy !

Will Murdock

Living in Fear

Race, Politics & The Republican Party
in South Carolina

WILL MOREDOCK

Selected Columns from Charleston City Paper

Copyright © 2015 Will Moredock
All rights reserved.
ISBN: 978-0-9723829-1-5
Library of Congress Control Number: 2014922465

Frontline Press, Ltd.
137 Hester Street
Charleston, South Carolina 29403
(843) 469-9137
www.frontlineltd.com
Design © Maryam Naderi 2015
This book was manufactured in the USA on recycled paper.

THIS BOOK IS DEDICATED TO MARYAM,
WHO, FOR BETTER, FOR WORSE, FOR RICHER, FOR POORER,
HAS MADE SOUTH CAROLINA HER HOME.

CONTENTS

FEAR & THE GOP

FEAR & VOTING

ACKNOWLEDGMENTS, APOLOGIES & EXPLANATIONS

In 2002, *Charleston City Paper* Editor Stephanie Barna asked me to write a weekly column on politics and public matters. Without that outlet and inspiration, this book would never have been written. Over the next ten years, my columns were gently edited by Stephanie and her successor, Chris Haire. I am very grateful to both.

A number of friends gave a reading and guidance on my opening essay, "300 Years of Living in Fear." They include Damon Fordham, Paul Garbarini, John Grooms, Stephen Hoffius, and Kerry Taylor. Another old friend, Floy Work, an English major of multiple talents and sensibilities, volunteered her time and attention to give this essay its final form.

Some will observe that my essay is not footnoted. First, let me say that it was written, like the columns which follow, for laypeople. The voice is casual, nonacademic. Much of it was cribbed from my columns and from ten years of mental notes and hand-written scraps of paper I collected in the course of researching these columns, as well as more general reading on South Carolina history, politics and culture. The point is that if writing this essay had been dependent upon reassembling all the sources I had used over many years, it would never have been done. Any guilt I may have felt over this lapse of scholarly standards vanished when I remembered that W.J. Cash used nary a footnote in his classic study, *The Mind of the South*.

Others, not familiar with the traditions and culture of alternative newspapers, may be surprised at the tone of some of these columns. They should understand that *Charleston City Paper*, like hundreds of alternative newsweekslies around the country, comes out of a tradition of irreverence spawned in the turbulent 1960s and early 1970s. Much of the rage and raunchiness that marked the genre 45 years ago has mellowed and matured, like the generation   that created it. Still, the alternative press is not your father's daily newspaper. Its use of expletives, sexual imagery and the like mark it as a different creature from the mainstream press. My columns, while tame compared to much *City Paper* fare, are part of the alternative newsweekly tradition.

On the matter of tone and language, readers may notice a tinge of anger in some of these columns. In editing these pieces, I decided not to dilute or delete that sentiment, for it is authentic and it reflects these angry partisan times we live in. Of course, some of my Internet readers expressed their anger at my opinions with their own posts. In fact, I considered calling this book *These Angry Times*. But as I drilled deeper on the subject, I remembered something else: the furious, inarticulate, uninformed screeds in capital letters and exclamation marks which many readers posted in response to some of my columns.

I had touched a nerve in the white southern anima which transcends politics and polemics. In writing on matters of race and its role through South Carolina history, I had struck a place so deep and personal with many white Southerners that they were incapable of articulating the pain or understanding where it came from. They could only flail away with as much violence and vehemence as their keystrokes would convey.

As a lifelong Southerner, as a South Carolinian born and bred, I recognized the impulse. They were reacting in fear and there was only one way for a traditional southern man, black or white, to meet fear. That is with violence – a sudden, mindless lashing out at the person or group that has threatened him. Not to respond immediately and forcefully is to be thought a coward – if only in one's own mind. And nothing is worse in the southern man's mind than the shame of cowardice. Preserving "honor" has caused countless men to kill and die without a moment's hesitation.

Threat and bluster and occasional violence are among the critical determinants of southern culture, but you don't have to call Dr. Freud to understand this is the behavior of people who are compensating for some deep insecurity. Violence is the impulsive expression of anger. And anger is the mask of fear.

One of the purposes of philosophy and religion is to understand the nature and the origin of evil. Jesus said the love of money is the root of all evil. In the mind of the Christian fundamentalist, lust is the source of most evil. Shakespeare suggested in plays, such as *Julius Caesar* and *Macbeth*, that unbridled ambition is the root of much of mankind's suffering.

For my money, fear is the greatest source of violence and hatred – both personal and collective: Fear of threats, real and imagined. Fear not only for our personal safety, but for our dignity, for our perceived place in the world and our relationships with others. Taken together, these things are what a traditional Southerner might call "honor."

Inside every abuser is a child afraid of losing control of his world. Inside every genocide is a fear of one group by another. Fear is the spirit that animates demagogues, mobs and witch hunts. It is not possible to understand the South without understanding the power of fear and all the ways it has been sublimated and manipulated over the centuries. This book is my attempt to explain the ways of fear in the place I know best in all the world: South Carolina.

300 YEARS OF LIVING IN FEAR

Unlike several of the English colonies of North America, South Carolina was not founded out of any lofty notion of providing religious freedom or sanctuary to debtors and miscreants. The ships which brought settlers into Charleston Harbor in 1670 also brought black slaves from the Caribbean. The settlers were from the English colony of Barbados, a small Caribbean island of sugar plantations, made possible only by the use of thousands of slaves. The Carolina colony was an attempt to bring the culture and economy of that overcrowded little island to the continental mainland.

Sugar cane was never profitably grown on the Carolina coast, but within a few generations Europeans were reaping great fortunes from rice, indigo and cotton. Those plantations required huge amounts of cheap labor, which could be supplied only by the African slave trade. By 1720, blacks outnumbered whites and would remain a majority for most of South Carolina's history. In the 1730s a visitor wrote that "Carolina looks more like a Negro Country than like a Country settled by white people."

To Europeans, the African was a mysterious creature, part child, part brute. He came from a strange and fabled continent and his skin was black, a color almost universally associated with death and evil among white Christians. And now these Africans outnumbered white Christians in the Carolina colony.

The first act of slave rebellion in South Carolina is not recorded, but we know it was a violent, futile gesture of human rage and despair. It may have involved one slave or several; it may have been spontaneous or planned. We don't know when or where it occurred, but we can be sure that it was suppressed quickly and brutally. The perpetrators may have been executed outright or tortured out of their minds. Whatever the penalty, it was done publicly, as much to terrorize other slaves as to punish the insurgents.

The history of Charleston over its first two centuries was one of periodic terror, followed by executions, curfews, and heightened police powers, all in an effort to regulate the enormous slave population. For white Southerners, slavery was more than an economic system. It was the only institution they could envision to control the seething slaves who surrounded and outnumbered them.

Today it is common to hear Confederate apologists declare that the Civil War was not fought over slavery, for only a small percentage of white Southerners were slaveholders. This statement is half true: indeed, relatively few whites owned slaves, but all white Southerners lived in silent dread of the black man and saw slavery as their only protection.

The fear of slave rebellion haunted white Southerners for generations. It was a terror which robbed them of sleep, shaped their politics and society, seeped into their subconscious and into the very marrow of their bones. Fear was as pervasive and debilitating as the summer heat.

From the earliest years of English colonization on the Atlantic seaboard, security against the African population dominated internal and external policy. No one has demonstrated this better than Herbert Aptheker in his classic study, *American Negro Slave Revolts*. In wars against Indians, French, Spanish, British, Mexicans and the northern states, a primary motivation was always to secure the borders against those who would foment revolt and offer shelter to a restless slave population. By the 1850s, southern expansionists were casting eyes on Mexico, Central America, Cuba, even Brazil – always with the purpose (or at least the pretext) of making the world safe for their "peculiar institution."

Aptheker cites generations of private and public correspondence, newspaper accounts, public records, legislation and other sources to demonstrate that the fear of servile insurrection was never far from the mind of southern whites.

The first recorded act of servile unrest in the Carolina colony occurred in 1702, when a slave "in Irons" was brought before the Commons House of Assembly in Charleston, accused of "threatening that he with other negroes would Rise and Cutt off the Inhabitants of this Province." The disposition of this case is not known.

In a 1711 address to the colonial Assembly, Governor Robert

Gibbs proposed an improved way to terrorize the burgeoning slave population by better displaying the bodies of executed insurgents: "...therefore, it might be convenient by some additional clause of said Negro Act to appoint either by gibbets or some such like way, that, after executed, they remain more exemplary, than any punishment hitherto has been inflicted on them."

Over the next decades, there were numerous small uprisings in and around Charleston, most of them put down quickly and brutally. Something close to guerrilla warfare existed on the outskirts of the colony, as bands of runaways attacked and plundered white farms, then disappeared into the forest. Other runaways fled south across Georgia, killing all whites they encountered on their way to Spanish Florida, where freedom and amnesty awaited them.

The bloodiest slave rebellion in British North America occurred on the Stono River, just south of Charleston, in September 1739. About eighty slaves went on a rampage, killing twenty-three whites and burning a path of some ten miles across the land as they moved toward Florida. When local militia overtook them, a short battle ensued. Several dozen rebels were killed; the rest were pursued for days and about forty captured, "who were immediately some shot, some hang'd and some Gibbeted alive." The dead slaves were decapitated, their heads placed on poles lining the road into Charleston.

The bloody affair left a mark on the white southern psyche: "... every breast was filled with concern..." wrote a contemporary. "Evil brought home to us within our very doors awakened the attention of the most unthinking."

The colonial legislature responded with the draconian Negro Code of 1740, which set harsh strictures on the freedom of slaves to move about and assemble, denied them the right to earn money or learn to write, gave owners the right to kill rebellious slaves if necessary. This law became the template for slave control in other southern colonies and states for over a century.

In June 1740, another large slave plot was exposed around Charleston. Authorities hanged fifty insurgents, in groups of ten a day, "to intimidate the other negroes."

Several fires burned through Charleston in 1740. A woman was condemned for arson in July, and a man was burned alive a few weeks later in another arson case. In 1754, two female slaves were burned in Charleston on charges of arson.

In a period of primitive medicine, when people died suddenly of mysterious causes, it was easy in a land of fear to believe that slaves were poisoning their owners' food or beverage. And slaves were periodically executed on this charge, with no evidence worthy of the term. In 1751, the South Carolina Assembly prescribed death without benefit of clergy to any slave convicted of poisoning. In 1761, the Charleston *Gazette* reported, "The negroes have again begun the hellish practice of poisoning." Eight years later, two black domestics were burned to death on the site of the future City Jail, on suspicion of having poisoned a white child.

In 1791, a rebellion broke out among slaves in the French Caribbean colony of Santo Domingo (now Haiti) and soon became a revolution. The war lasted a decade, with blacks and whites slaughtering one another in unspeakable savagery. During that time, southern states were rife with speculation that Haitian armies or agents were on their way to foment revolt among American slaves.

Aptheker cites an account in a New York newspaper from 1793: "They write from Charleston (S.C.) that the NEGROES have become very insolent, in so much as the citizens are alarmed, and the militia keep a constant guard. It is said that the St. Domingo negroes have sown these seeds of revolt...."

There was a series of fires in Charleston in the spring of 1796. A citizen wrote: "People seemed afraid to inquire into it – some would whisper their opinion that the negroes of the place were the authors; others that the French negroes were and that they certainly intended to make a St. Domingo business of it."

There were more arsons, more uprisings, more executions throughout the 1790s. When the decade ended, white Carolinians looked south in horror at a new republic of former slaves on their virtual doorstep. And they added to their lexicon two words which were essence and code for their deepest fears: Santo Domingo.

As fear of servile insurrection deepened, South Carolina, like other southern states, occasionally took measures to stop or curtail the importation of slaves. But soon wealthy planters were crying for more labor and their influence outweighed any consideration for public safety. The gates were flung open once again to the slavemongers, as Southerners weighed the balance between fear and greed.

In 1804, a plot was betrayed and some dozen leaders seized, tried and hanged. "Their heads were cut off, stuck on poles and set up along the highway leading from Purrysburg, the place of the trial, to Coosawhatchie..."

In 1808, a Massachusetts resident wrote home from Charleston: "There has not been a night this week without alarms and fires and murders; and the panic has become so great they were last night obliged to order three detachments of Infantry and part of the horse from several companies to guard the city..."

A large conspiracy was thwarted in Camden, in July 1816. A resident wrote to a friend in Philadelphia: "Our gaol is filled with negroes...This is really a dreadful situation to be in – I think it is time for us to leave a country where we cannot go to bed in safety. Their thirst for revenge must have been very great..." Six slaves were hanged for that plot. In 1831, a fire, thought to have been started by slaves, destroyed 85 buildings in Camden.

In 1822, the Denmark Vesey plot was uncovered in Charleston, along with the purported plans to murder the white population of the city. As reported by authorities, the fanciful details of this alleged conspiracy included putting the rebellious slaves on ships in Charleston harbor and sailing them away to Santo Domingo.

Not a shot was fired, not a weapon discovered, nor a drop of blood shed. Some modern historians believe the conspiracy story was concocted by white authorities, justifying a mass execution to terrorize a "sassy" black population into abject subservience. Whatever the reality, more than thirty slaves and freedmen were marched up beyond present day Marion Square and hanged.

There were several immediate outcomes of the Denmark Vesey incident. First, the City of Charleston petitioned the state Assembly to create a "citadel" in the city to serve as an arsenal and muster point for militia. Such was the genesis of the modern military school now located on the banks of Ashley River.

Also, the city instituted a system of mounted street patrols, with regular beats and schedules, to stop and question any suspicious or unauthorized persons. This was the beginning of the modern police department.

And finally, the state legislature answered the fears of white citizens with the Negro Seaman's Act of 1823. Under this law, any free person of color entering Charleston harbor on a ship of any nationality would have to surrender himself to local authorities and be incarcerated in the city Work House while his ship was in South Carolina waters. While incarcerated, the seaman or his captain would be responsible for paying for his upkeep. If payment were not made, the seaman could be sold to pay his obligations.

The Negro Seaman's Act violated United States and international law and sparked outrage on both sides of the Atlantic. But such was the terror in the white population that any amount of scorn could be endured in the name of security.

In the decades before the Civil War, there were countless smaller uprisings and acts of defiance. Alexis de Tocqueville traveled through the young nation – including South Carolina – in 1831, observing American society for his great study, *Democracy in America*. There he wrote that although the fear of slave insurrection "perpetually haunts the imagination of Americans," white Southerners generally faced the prospect with "frightening ... silence."

In 1831 came the Nat Turner rebellion in Southampton, Virginia. Several dozen slaves, led by Turner, unleashed their fury on their owners and any other whites they came upon, killing approximately sixty people, before they were stopped two days later by a combination of militias and federal forces. Local militia units went on a rampage, killing between 100 and 200 innocent slaves. Fifty-seven insurgents were ultimately tried and hanged.

The uprising sparked something close to hysteria across the region. South Carolina newspapers added to the panic, running gruesome accounts of the killing. In the wake of the Nat Turner rebellion, a Charlestonian wrote that it would take only the slightest encouragement for belligerent slaves to "lay the firebrand to our houses and the daggers to our throats," and Charleston Mayor Henry Laurens Pinckney denounced the abolitionist movement, saying it "whets the knife and lights the torch of insurrection."

In *The Peculiar Institution,* Kenneth M. Stampp describes the effect of the Nat Turner rebellion on the white southern mind: "Thus ended an event which produced in the South something resembling a mass trauma, from which the whites had not recovered three decades later...the fear of rebellion, sometimes vague, sometimes acute, was with them always....Whether caused by rumor or fact, the specter of rebellion often troubled the sleep of the master class. The Turner rebellion itself produced an insurrection panic that swept the entire South....A South Carolinian reported that there was 'considerable alarm' in his state...and that some slaves were hanged to prevent a rumored uprising."

Across the Deep South – and especially in South Carolina – the public orthodoxy on slavery hardened into rigid intolerance. No discussion of emancipation was allowed in the public forum. Some politicians called for the death penalty for anyone advocating abolition. There was a law against hiring Northerners as teachers in any school, for fear they might instill sedition. Governor and Senator James H. Hammond wrote to a northern correspondent, "What we do fear is your abolitionist emissaries who, like the Serpent in Eden, whisper *lies*. We hang all of them we can catch."

To control their huge slave populations, southern states became police states. Visitors in the South commented on the militarism they saw everywhere. Militia units mustered and drilled in almost every southern town. In the countryside were slave patrols: men on horseback who policed the rural roads, looking for any slave traveling without papers, any gathering of slaves or other suspicious activity. Slave patrols operated with no legal process, seizing, whipping and terrorizing any suspicious slave on a whim. Almost all adult white men were subject to patrol duty. White Southerners gladly traded their personal freedom for personal security from their slaves.

In Charleston, in 1835, it became known that northern anti-slavery tracts were in the federal post office, awaiting distribution throughout the South. A mob descended on the building, seized the offending tracts and destroyed them in a great bonfire on Marion Square. Also in that year, three white men were lynched in Aiken on suspicion of fomenting a slave uprising.

In 1853-54, Frederick Law Olmsted traveled through much of the South to write a series of articles for the *New York Daily Times*. He observed in Charleston that

> ...one sees police machinery such as you never find in towns under free government: citadels, sentries, passports, grapeshotted cannon and daily public whippings of the subjects for accidental infractions of police ceremonies. I happened myself to see more direct expression of tyranny in a single day and night in Charleston, than in Naples in a week; and I found that more than half the inhabitants of this town were subject to arrest, imprisonment, and barbarous punishment, if found in the streets without a passport after the evening 'gunfire.' Similar precautions and similar customs may be discovered in every large town in the South... There is...nearly everywhere in [the South] always prepared to act, if not always in service, an armed force, with a military organization, which is invested with more arbitrary and cruel power than any police in Europe.

By 1859, southern tempers were short, southern nerves frayed by decades of slave unrest and the fears and rumors they bred. In that year John Brown led his hapless band of true-believers in their raid at Harpers Ferry, hoping to spark a great rebellion. They failed, of course, but they accomplished something else. In *Crisis of Fear – Secession in South Carolina*, Stephen Channing writes: "With unconscious insight John Brown had struck at the deepest and most intimate anxieties of the white South. The fear and rage he had aroused were at the heart of the secession movement."

The election of Abraham Lincoln in November 1860 was the last provocation the radicals of South Carolina would endure. Lincoln was not an abolitionist and the Republican platform in 1860 was not an abolitionist agenda. But it did call for restricting slavery from the western territories. South Carolina "fire-eaters" used this fact, and the triumph of the Republican Party, as evidence that slavery would soon be abolished and slaves unleashed upon the land. National leaders did what they could to assuage such fears, but Southerners, particularly in South Carolina, were beyond rational thought.

Channing writes: "...the conclusion is inescapable that the multiplicity of fears revolving around the maintenance of race controls for the Negro was not simply the prime concern for the people of South Carolina in their revolution, but was so very vast and frightening that it literally consumed the lesser 'causes' of secession which have inspired historians."

In the wake of the election, polemicists such as South Carolina clergyman James C. Furman whipped his fellow Baptists into a frenzy with screeds warning of the prospect of abolition: "Then every negro in South Carolina and every other Southern state will be his own master, nay, more than that, will be the equal of every one of you. If you are tame enough to submit, Abolition preachers will be at hand to consummate the marriage of your daughters to black husbands."

The election of Lincoln, James H. Hammond wrote in a letter to the state legislature in November 1860, was "no mere political or ethical conflict, but a social conflict in which there will be a war of races, to be waged at midnight with the torch, the knife & poison."

With rising sectional tensions, slaves throughout the South became restless, sensing their moment was at hand. Channing quotes an Abbeville District woman who wrote to her sister in December 1860, assuring her that the slave patrols were at work and all was well. But a suspected abolitionist had been captured, she wrote and "an alarming plot" had been discovered in the area. "Five negroes are to be hung, twenty white men implicated..."

On December 20, 1860, delegates assembled in Charleston voted unanimously to take South Carolina out of the Union. Over the next five months, ten other southern states followed. In the weeks immediately after secession, some South Carolinians living and traveling outside the state expressed hesitation to return home, for fear the place would soon explode in servile insurrection.

· From the outset of the Civil War, Union leaders understood that the slave population was their "fifth column" against the Confederacy. One of the first Union incursions onto Confederate territory was the invasion of Port Royal, South Carolina, in November 1861. Port Royal was chosen in part because slaves outnumbered whites nearly ten-to-one. When federal troops landed, the white population fled inland as the slaves rushed to the Union lines. Within a year, former slaves around Port Royal were being armed and trained to fight in the Union Army.

Of the role of slaves in the Civil War, historian Joseph E. Holloway has written:

> In fact, it is possible to say that enslaved Africans contributed directly to their own liberation by rebelling and participating in insurrectionary activities. ...Ultimately, the fear of internal collapse from widespread slave revolts affected the South externally and contributed both to the demise of slavery and the collapse of the Confederacy. African Americans recognized in the war an opportunity to destabilize the regime from within by revolt...
>
> This anxiety placed a great pressure upon both the national and state governments of the Confederacy to divert a substantial proportion of the South's war-making resources to maintaining the social control of the plantation system. The inability of the South to control slave labor while simultaneously fighting for independence undermined Confederate unity, limited the Confederacy's ability to execute the war, and led to the decomposition of the plantation system itself....

The end of the Civil War brought the end of slavery, and with it the end of servile insurrection and the terror it created in the hearts of white people. In the two and a half centuries of slavery in English-speaking America, there were thousands of acts of defiance and rebellion, large and small, recorded and lost to history. With the exception of a relatively few slaves who escaped to the North and to Spanish Florida, all of these acts had one thing in common: they failed.

Holloway describes these acts poignantly: "The revolts were all doomed from the start, and yet slaves still revolted against insurmountable odds in the fight for their personal freedom and liberty."

The postbellum world brought new fears and anxieties for southern whites. Now their former slaves were free to own property, establish businesses, vote and hold public office. They were no longer subservient, but were rivals – politically, economically, and perhaps most terrifying to white males, sexually.

The end of slavery was little more than a legalism in the minds of white Southerners. Their ideology of white supremacy was implacable. Their need to control was as strong as ever. With slavery gone, whites resorted to new means of imposing order in a biracial society. They turned to Jim Crow laws and the discreet use of terror and violence, such as lynching and paramilitary organizations like the Ku Klux Klan.

After the war, federal forces occupied the former Confederate states; the Thirteenth, Fourteenth, and Fifteenth Amendments to the U.S. Constitution were passed, giving former slaves citizenship and males the right to vote. With their new citizenship and political power, and with Republican allies from the North, African Americans organized and ran the state governments in the South.

White Southerners found the situation humiliating and intolerable. As white males regained their citizenship and their right to vote, they took control of their state governments, dismantling the black Reconstruction governments that ruled over them. They were aided by local paramilitary organizations composed of former Confederate soldiers. This was especially true in South Carolina. In fact, a white return to power might have been impossible without violence, because blacks composed some sixty percent of the population.

As the election of 1876 approached, the paramilitaries began recruiting, training, drilling and mustering around the state. Contemporary South Carolinian Belton O'Neall Townsend observed the preparations for a race war as his state became an armed camp leading up to the election:

...100,000 revolvers and Winchester and Remington breach-loading rifles have been imported into the state during the past two months; ... a dozen batteries of artillery have been brought; ... 75,000 whites, men and boys, are under arms – of whom 45,000 are trained veterans from the Confederate army, admirably equipped, organized not only in [rifle] clubs, companies, battalions and regiments, but with officers who, from the sergeants, lieutenants, and captains up to the majors, colonels and generals, have already long borne military titles obtained not by service in the militia, but on the fields of Manassas, Malvern Hill and Gettysburg...

White militias broke up black political meetings, attacked black communities and leaders, and murdered scores. The most notorious incident to come out of that season of blood was the Hamburg Massacre of July 1876. There an extra-legal white militia contrived a conflict with an authorized black militia. Hundreds of armed white men descended on Hamburg from miles around. In the battle that followed, one white and several blacks were killed. About forty blacks surrendered and were rounded up. Six leaders were called out by name and executed.

The election that November was marked by massive voter fraud on both sides, but whites carried the day with their terror and organized violence. Democrat Wade Hampton III was elected governor. Negotiations in Washington led to the withdrawal of federal troops from South Carolina and Reconstruction ended. Whites returned to power and began the process of removing African Americans from office, stripping them of voting rights, of legal protections and of all personal dignity.

One of the leaders of the white militia – they were called Red Shirts – was a young Edgefield farmer named Benjamin Ryan Tillman. Tillman would go on to become governor and United States senator. In 1895, he called, then orchestrated a constitutional convention in Columbia, the primary purpose of which was to remove African Americans from the voter rolls and do it without disenfranchising poor, white voters, yet do it in such a manner as not to alarm federal authorities to a wholesale violation of the Fourteenth

Amendment. Speaking on the floor of the Senate in 1900, Tillman apologized for nothing that he and his followers had done:

> In my State there were 135,000 negro voters, or negroes of voting age, and some 90,000 or 95,000 white voters. General Canby set up a carpetbag government there and turned our State over to this majority. Now, I want to ask you, with a free vote and a fair count, how are you going to beat 135,000 by 95,000? How are you going to do it? You had set us an impossible task....
>
> We did not disfranchise the negroes until 1895. Then we had a constitutional convention convened which took the matter up calmly, deliberately, and avowedly with the purpose of disfranchising as many of them as we could under the fourteenth and fifteenth amendments. We adopted the educational qualification as the only means left to us, and the negro is as contented and as prosperous and as well protected in South Carolina today as in any State of the Union south of the Potomac.... We of the South have never recognized the right of the negro to govern white men, and we never will. We have never believed him to be equal to the white man...

With blacks removed from the voter rolls, they were soon removed from the General Assembly and other elective offices. The white legislature then set about imposing a brutal form of apartheid on the state. Similar laws were passed across the South. They were called Jim Crow laws and their purpose was to deny African Americans access to decent education, jobs, capital, cultural and intellectual resources. With blacks so reduced in power and assets, they were no longer a threat to whites.

The late nineteenth century, with its rapid urbanization and industrialization, was a frightening time in many ways, as traditional values and relationships were challenged by new wealth, new sources of power, new ideas about the nature of god and man. These threats were compounded in the South with the social upheaval unleashed by Emancipation and the end of the old agrarian plutocracy. Jim Crow was an attempt on the part of white Southerners to reestablish order, especially the ideology of white supremacy.

Among the many laws passed in South Carolina were statutes forbidding interracial marriage and interracial sexual relations. Of course, it was understood by the white men who passed these laws that they would apply only to black men having relationships with white women. For centuries, white men had used the legal and material power of slavery to force themselves on black women.

With slavery ended, black men had both the legal right and the means to defend their homes and their women from white interposition. Furthermore, free black men owning their own land and businesses could become rivals for the attentions of white women. Jim Crow laws were created to eliminate that possibility, to keep black people – especially black men – poor and powerless.

Fear of the black man was never far from the consciousness of whites. Before 1865, it was – like violence itself – an inevitable byproduct of slavery. After 1865 – and especially after the end of Reconstruction – fear became a political commodity, planted, cultivated and harvested by the Democratic Party, like so much cotton or rice.

The most powerful weapon the white establishment used against blacks was the image of the black man as predator and rapist of white women. At various times and places throughout the South prior to 1900, there were attempts to lure poor white farmers away from the Democratic Party and into the ranks of the Republican and Populist parties, which challenged the dominance of Democrats. Democrats maintained white solidarity through raw fear, telling poor whites that the politics of "racial fusion" was a subterfuge to give black men access to white women. In her book, *Gender & Jim Crow*, historian Glenda Elizabeth Gilmore explained how the "black rapist" gambit was played in North Carolina:

> In 1898, the Democrats chose Furnifold Simmons to orchestrate the campaign to recapture a majority in the state legislature....He chose to make protection of white women the centerpiece of the campaign. By emphasizing sexuality, the Democrats placed race over class and spun a yarn in which white women of all classes highly prized their chastity and black men of all classes barely controlled their sexuality. By positing lust for white wom-

en as a universal trait of black men, whites explained away black [men's] good behavior by arguing that they sought success simply to get close to white women....Black progress of any sort meant a move toward social equality, a code word for sexual equality....

To turn black [men] from politics and corral white Populist strays, Simmons, Aycock, and Daniels in 1898 created a local black-on-white rape scare, taking their cue from similar sensational reporting across the South. By the time they finished, they had racialized the definition of manhood and substituted race for class....Rhetorically, if not literally, Democrats embraced poor whites across class lines and politicized poor white men's personal lives, destroying the fragile black/white political alliance that had emerged with the Populist Party. The political machine exaggerated a series of sex crimes and allegations in order to strike terror into the hearts of white voters....The evidence suggests that the Democratic propaganda planted seeds of hysteria that ripened in the minds of an economically threatened people...

The Democrats charged that while white men slumbered, the incubus of black power visited their beds. They summed up their platform as 'safety of the home.' Democratic rule would 'restore to the white women of the state the security they felt under [previous Democratic administration].'

Historians have noted that the rape hysteria swept the South in the decades just before and after the turn of the last century – the very years when the Democratic Party was wresting control of state governments from black voters and officeholders, and re-imposing the rule of white supremacy. There had been no scourge of black-on-white rape during the Civil War, when so many white males were away from home, fighting at the front; no scourge of black-on-white rape during Reconstruction, when black Republicans ran southern state governments and much of law enforcement.

Throughout the South, rape or attempted rape was generally treated as a capital offense – especially when it involved a black man and a white woman. But with rising frequency, terrified whites were not satisfied to allow a judge and jury to convict and sentence an accused rapist. Mobs of angry whites began lynching black men accused of rape, attempted rape or some lesser offense – real or imagined – against a white woman. The sexual significance – and the sexual fear – behind the act is emphasized by the fact that lynching victims were periodically castrated, before or after death. But in fact, the practice of lynching had nothing to do with protecting white womanhood and everything to do with enforcing white supremacy.

Between 1882 and 1930, there were an estimated 2,805 lynchings across the South; 156 of those took place in South Carolina.

White South Carolina politicians enthusiastically endorsed the practice. Ben Tillman declared on the floor of the Senate: "We have never believed [the black man] to be equal to the white man, and we will not submit to his gratifying his lust on our wives and daughters without lynching him."

Governor Cole Blease (1911-1915) infamously said, "Whenever the Constitution comes between me and the virtue of the white women of South Carolina, I say, 'to hell with the Constitution.'"

Lynchings gradually declined and had almost vanished from the cultural landscape by the end of World War II. (The last lynching in South Carolina took place in 1947.) But by the end of the 1940s, there was a new threat to white people's sense of equanimity. The civil rights movement was in its infancy. And for the first time since Reconstruction, the federal government was coming down on the side of black people. And like Reconstruction, it threatened the pillars of white supremacy, the power and the privilege of the white man in all political, economic and personal relationships.

Federal court decisions in 1947 and 1948 opened South Carolina's "white primary" to African-Americans. In February 1948, President Harry Truman integrated the Armed Forces by executive order and that summer the Democratic National Convention adopted a civil rights plank in its national platform. Southern Democrats responded by seceding from the Democratic Party and briefly forming the States Rights or Dixiecrat Party, with South Carolina Governor Strom Thurmond as its presidential candidate. The Dixiecrats carried only a handful of Deep South states, but it marked the beginning of the end for the Solid South, as white people began to shift their allegiance from the Democratic Party.

In 1950, black parents in Clarendon County, with the backing of the NAACP, filed a federal suit against the county school district, seeking equal access to education for their children. The case of *Briggs v. Elliott* made its way through the courts until it arrived at the U.S. Supreme Court. There it was consolidated with four similar cases from other states and given the name of the case from Kansas: *Brown v. Board of Education of Topeka*. In 1954, the Supreme Court handed down its monumental decision, ruling segregation in public schools unconstitutional. Thus began decades of sometimes violent white resistance to desegregation.

The school desegregation battle launched a whole new generation of white fears and white demagogues. One of their favorite tropes was the image of the black boy and the white girl going to school together and the dreadful consequences that would surely ensue. One of the great cliches and rhetorical questions on the lips of countless white people in that era was, "How would you like your daughter/sister to marry one?"

In March 1970, about 200 angry white people in rural Lamar, in Darlington County, gathered to protest a recent federal desegregation order. They were armed with axe handles, bricks and chains. Nine days earlier, demagogue and Republican congressman Albert Watson had harangued a white rally in Lamar. According to journalist Jack Bass, Watson told the mob to "stand up and use every means at your disposal to defend [against] what I consider to be an illegal order of the Circuit Court of the United States." Explaining why he traveled from his Columbia-based district to speak to angry protesters in Lamar, he said, "Those citizens are interested in their children and I will stand with them."

Of course, the children he referred to were white and the citizens of his concern – like the white citizens of South Carolina nearly half a century later – did not care that their children attended some of the worst schools in the nation, did not care that their children had among the worst diets and healthcare in the nation, did not care that their children suffered one of the highest infant mortality rates or rates of violence and disease in the nation. These conditions had been part of South Carolina's social landscape for so many generations that they were politically irrelevant then, as they are today. But the thought of putting their white children on buses with black children, the thought of those white and black children sitting together in the same classrooms so terrified the white people of Lamar, that on March 3, 1970, the mob attacked and overturned two school buses that had just delivered black children to schools in the town.

Over the years, civil rights activists have been beaten, burned out, economically ruined, even murdered by frightened white people who could not imagine a world of racial equality. It was too alien, too threatening to all they had ever known and understood. They have been fighting against it for generations and they are fighting against it still.

Fear. It is a primal and atavistic part of us, essential to our survival. Like pain and hunger, it preserves the individual and the species by generating a survival response to danger. In the jungle and on the savanna, primates with a more keenly developed sense of fear were more likely to survive, reproduce, and pass this trait to their offspring.

Psychologists have long understood the nexus of fear and anger. Fear manifests itself in numerous ways, including anger, violence, and the need to control. Fear brings out the dark side of democracy. It distorts reality and relationships. The leader who pounds on the table, who points and shouts and screams is perceived as powerful and knowledgeable. He identifies groups and individuals who must be dealt with. He explains history and society without nuance or complexity. Likewise, the angry individual will see the world in terms of discreet and simple problems, which can be solved quickly and easily with direct action.

In human society, fear is the enemy of comity, personal freedom, political and cultural diversity. It fosters authoritarianism, intolerance, mass conformity, and a counter-factual world view. And fear has been the driving force behind southern politics and culture for centuries. Nothing so distorts and undermines a free society as fear. It can be generated by outside elements during a period of war or international strife. But it can also be generated by internal elements – real or imagined. Such fear is often used by politicians and social antagonists to create a general state of anxiety and alarm.

External wars eventually end, allowing a society to return to what Warren G. Harding called a state of "normalcy." This is at least true of victorious nations in war. For the losers, things are often quite different. The war might go on for generations in the minds of their people – warping their politics and society, making them intolerant, authoritarian, delusional in their view of history and the world. (See France after 1871, Germany after 1918.)

This is what happened to the South. Not only has the white population been in a permanent state of siege against its black population for centuries, but it lost a devastating war against the North, a loss many white Southerners still have not come to terms with.

It might be useful here to briefly compare the history and culture of the South to the history and culture of New England and California. When English settlers first arrived in Massachusetts in the early seventeenth century, they were terrified of the vast, dense forest and the natives who dwelled there. They had several brutal wars with the Native Americans, but by the beginning of the eighteenth century the natives were vanquished and the settlers had secured their place on the continent. They learned to clear the trees to make way for fields. They discovered that the once forbidding forest was wealth waiting to be harvested to build ships and houses.

With the exception of a brief occupation of Boston by British forces before the Revolutionary War, New England would never again face any foreign or domestic threat to its security. And because it was secure, it was free to develop into the crown jewel of American civilization, producing some of America's greatest universities, writers, artists and thinkers.

Something similar happened in California. The Gold Rush brought tens of thousands of people to that remote land in only two years. The small groups of Native Americans who had lived there were quickly vanquished, as were any remnants of Mexican resistance to Anglo supremacy. In California, the frontier was closed almost immediately. California has never faced any serious threat to its security since that day. It, like New England, has been free to develop some of the finest universities in the world, some of the most important technologies and entertainments of the past century.

The South, by contrast, at least the white South, has lived under constant siege against an internal foe – its black population. The siege has lasted for centuries, along with the concomitant state of fear and repression which war demands of its participants. And because the South has remained in a psychological state of war, it has remained a cultural frontier – violent, intolerant, and anti-intellectual, as all frontiers are.

The southern frontier has never closed. In his masterpiece, *Haunted by God*, South Carolina farmer and philosopher James McBride Dabbs describes the "effect of the black racial frontier upon the whites who lived along it."

Dabbs wrote: "...the racial frontier was everywhere, wherever a black man was, or from the black man's point of view, wherever a white man was. For each thought the other, because of his race, to some degree strange, unknown, unpredictable. 'That's just like a nigger,' said the white, uncomprehending. 'White folks is white folks,' said the black, shaking his head."

Whites feared blacks, Dabbs wrote: "....they feared them because of their superficial strangeness, a strangeness which whites often refused to understand in order that they might hide from their own eyes their exploitative activity."

The frontier has been there for centuries, in the mind and heart of every Southerner, black and white. It is usually quiet these days, but the "combatants" eye one another across the front daily – on the street, in the work place, over the service counter. There is little evidence of the blood and fury which marked this frontier for generations, though blacks have more social memory of that ugly past than whites, just as white Southerners are still obsessed with the Civil War, a conflict many northerners regard as a quaint historic curiosity.

In the twenty-first century, the South is changing rapidly and almost everyone – even the most recalcitrant conservatives – agrees that it should change. The question white Southerners must answer in the next generation is whether there is anything of the old South worth saving. It does have its charm, even its virtues, as W.J. Cash wrote in *The Mind of the South*: "Proud, brave, honorable by it lights, courteous, personally generous, loyal, swift to act, often too swift, but signally effective, sometimes terrible in its action – such was the South at its best." Yet, there is another South, which he also acknowledged: "Violence, intolerance, aversion, and suspicion toward new ideas, an incapacity for analysis, an inclination to act from feeling rather than thought, an exaggerated individualism and a too narrow concept of social responsibility, attachment to fictions and false values, above all, too great attachment to racial values and a tendency to justify cruelty and injustice in the name of those values, sentimentality and lack of realism – these have been its characteristic values in the past."

Too great attachment to racial values. For centuries, every public issue and perhaps most private relationships were viewed through the prism of race. Driving all of these considerations has been fear.

Irrational fear poisons individuals, personal relationships, whole societies. To fear death, to fear strangers, to fear the unknown is perfectly human – and usually irrational. It is an adult's responsibility to overcome these fears, to act rationally in public affairs and courageously in private matters.

Even when fear is rational, it is a primitive instinct, the emotional equivalent of a stone club or a sharpened stick. It can be useful for survival, but nothing beautiful was ever built of fear. Yet fear has been the primary building block of southern society and culture for centuries. Out of fear, white Southerners have created a violent, authoritarian society.

To heal the South, to bring peace to its troubled soul and light to its darkened mind, it is necessary to understand the poison which has infected it for so many generations. That poison is fear – ancient, primordial, racial fear. And until we come to recognize that fear, in ourselves and others, all the laws and arguments for justice and progress will be for naught.

Southern white people must understand what African Americans have known in their stoic hearts for centuries. By whatever means, for whatever reason, fate has cast us up together on this shore where we must spend eternity, side by side. Gated communities, private schools and clubs are only superficial shelter to the white psyche.

After these centuries together, our folkways and foodways, our speech and music, our very blood is intermingled and in inseparable. Whether we live in peace and prosperity or in strife and scarcity is largely the choice of white people, who make the laws, control the economy and dominate the culture. For nearly four centuries whites have chosen strife and scarcity over peace and prosperity. They have acted largely out of fear – fear of African Americans, fear of people and ideas which threaten the awkward and painful relationship between the races. Whites have succeeded in holding black people down, but they have done so at great cost to themselves.

There is a saying in the black community: You can stand over me with your foot on my neck, but you cannot go anywhere with your foot on my neck. And, in fact, the South has not gone far in the last two centuries. It has been socially and economically paralyzed, to the detriment of all. Martin Luther King Jr. said that the civil rights movement would do more than free black people. It would free white people to be their best selves and fulfill their greatest potential. But before that can happen, the white people of the South must face themselves, face the future and free themselves from fear.

Read this and other essays online at livinginfearbook.com.

FEAR & RACE

"I want to tell you, ladies and gentlemen, that there's not enough troops in the Army to force the southern people to break down segregation and admit the Negro race into our theaters, into our swimming pools, into our homes, and into our churches."

— Gov. Strom Thurmond,
Dixiecrat presidential candidate, 1948

FAIR COMMENT
STILL DEALING WITH RACIST SYMBOLS IN PUBLIC PLACES

A few decades ago traveling carnivals, such as the Coastal Carolina Fair, were a very different kind of entertainment. Sure, there were the rides and games, the wonderful food, the bright lights and crowds.

It was all there, but there was something else. There were the "freak shows," featuring dwarfs and the two-headed calf, the Tattooed Lady and the 800-Pound Man, and "More! More! More!" as the barker broadcast from the front of the tent.

And there was more. I'm talking about the "hoochie-koochie" girls, who took their clothes off to entertain the swains, farmers, and mill hands in the heart of Jesus country.

Over the years, the freaks and the strippers were sent packing as traveling carnivals made themselves more family-friendly. But clearly there's still work to be done, as the recent spat over racist T-shirts at the Coastal Carolina Fair demonstrated.

To recap: A vendor was selling shirts featuring Confederate flags and the words, "Confederately Correct Civil Rights for Southern Whites." When Deanna Bernstein saw the T-shirts, her "stomach turned," she told the *Post and Courier*. She asked the vendor to remove the shirts from view, then requested fair officials to take action. Both refused, so Bernstein staged a one-woman protest at the entrance of the fair and was arrested for trespassing.

After the initial report, the *P&C* received an astonishing amount of hate mail and phone calls directed at Bernstein. Some of it was focused on the fact that she is from California and has a Jewish name. Bernstein also received hate mail, phone calls, and threats at her home.

One of the e-mails to the *P&C* was from a man who identified himself as commander of the American National Socialist Workers (Nazi) Party, who wrote, "The only tragedy in this case is that her count of trespassing doesn't carry a sentence of execution. Lynching her and burning her home in the manner of the Union armies she so loves would set a just example for the community."

What can we make of this T-shirt flap?

Chip Boling, president of the Coastal Carolina Fair, said that Bernstein was warned that no political demonstrations or activities were allowed on the fairgrounds. Bernstein was arrested when she refused to stop her protest. Boling somehow determined that the T-shirt in question, with references to race, history, and civil rights, was not a political statement, but Bernstein's protest was.

It is impossible for an aware and reasonable person to not find this T-shirt offensive. Assuming the shirt might have slipped the notice of Boling and his staff, Bernstein's complaint should have resulted in its prompt removal. The fact that Boling did not act says much about him.

The *P&C* featured Chip Boling in one of its High Profile stories on October 28. He came across as an affable rube, a farmer by birth and career. His regular job is with the Clemson Extension service, where I would wager 99 percent of his colleagues and co-workers are white.

As a member of the Exchange Club — which he extolled for its "patriotism and Americanism" — Boling was tapped to head the Coastal Carolina Fair. He may be a great farmer, great patriot, and great American, but he clearly is not equipped to deal with the nuances of public policy in a multicultural fishbowl like the Coastal Carolina Fair. He has probably gotten away with this kind of crap down on the farm all his life and never thought twice about it, but he was in the spotlight at CCF and he blew it. Let's hope someone else is calling the shots at the fairgrounds next year.

How could an incident like this have happened in 2006?

Three days after Bernstein was arrested at the fairgrounds, America went to the polls. From coast to coast, voters replaced Republicans with Democrats in congressional and statehouse races. Even in Virginia, North Carolina, Georgia, and Florida Democrats picked up a U.S. Senate seat and several House seats. But in South Carolina, not only did Republicans hold onto all their congressional seats; they increased their hold on statewide executive offices.

This violent, ill-tempered little state continues to live in fear of the future, of black people, of multiculturalism. The white majority lashes out at all three with their Confederate flag, their racist T-shirts, their angry letters to local newspapers. And they lash out with their lockstep subordination to the Republican Party. The GOP remains the White People's Party, a perfect index of this state's sublimated white supremacy. And as long as the Republicans keep their death grip on state politics and culture, we will continue to have embarrassments like the recent incident at the Coastal Carolina Fair.

November 22, 2006

LIVING IN FEAR
A LITTLE HISTORY LESSON TO EXPLAIN HOW WE GOT HERE

White Southerners love their rights. They've got state's rights and property rights and individual rights. They've got sacred rights and god-given rights. They've got rights out the wazoo. But one thing you will rarely hear a white Southerner speak for is his civil rights.

That's because whites long ago signed over their civil rights, accepting a virtual police state in exchange for a little security.

For nearly half of its history, South Carolina has had a black majority -- first a majority of slaves, later a majority of free blacks. (In 1860, the population was 61 percent black -- the largest majority of any state.) To control and preserve this huge, restless population of bondsmen was the first priority of all public policy in the state. The fear of slave revolt haunted white Southerners for generations. It was a terror which robbed them of sleep, shaped their politics and society, seeped into the subconscious and into the very marrow of white Southerners. Fear was as pervasive and debilitating as the summer heat.

South Carolina's bloodiest slave rebellion occurred on the Stono River, south of Charleston, in 1739. In 1822, the Denmark Vesey plot was uncovered -- along with the purported plans to murder the white population of Charleston. Not a shot was actually fired, but more than 30 slaves and freedmen were hanged for their roles in the alleged conspiracy. Between the Stono Rebellion and the Vesey conspiracy was the bloody Haitian revolution, which threw off French rule and established a republic of freed slaves in the Caribbean. Along the way were countless smaller uprisings in South Carolina and throughout the slave-holding region.

To control the slave population, Southern states established slave patrols to ride the roads and interrogate anyone -- black or white -- who looked suspicious. Local authorities opened the U.S. mail when they suspected abolitionist material was being sent into the state. These and numerous other violations of civil rights were taken for granted by whites as the price of security.

Fear of losing control of their slaves eventually drove the South to secession. After the disastrous war, they sought to impose control over their former slaves through Jim Crow laws and lynching. The new fear was of blacks gaining political power. And, of course, there was the ancient fear of miscegenation, which haunted the white man's sleep.

In the face of the civil rights movement, it was generally understood that anyone who worked for social change could be terrorized or murdered with impunity. Local authorities would not lift a hand to protect civil rights workers, resulting in the murder of dozens of activists, black and white. The State of Mississippi even created a secret, state-funded police bureaucracy worthy of the old Soviet KGB. The Mississippi Sovereignty Commission opened mail, tapped phones, and paid neighbors and coworkers to spy on suspected "agitators." No invasion of privacy, no abridgement of civil rights was too egregious, as long as it was done in the name of white supremacy.

The culture of fear was so endemic that it spilled over into virtually all aspects of life -- fear of communists, fear of intellectuals, fear of any outsider or new idea. The most hated institutions in the region were the National Association for the Advancement of

Colored People and the American Civil Liberties Union, for challenging some of the South's most pernicious laws.

Generations of white politicians cultivated the politics of fear into an art form. Men like the late Strom Thurmond could denounce the NAACP, the ACLU, the Supreme Court, and "godless communism" in one bombastic breath. And his white audience was happy to believe him.

Today, the Republican Party keeps white Southerners transfixed in their fear of terrorism and gays, and their fear keeps them snugly in the pocket of George W. Bush.

This shabby history comes to mind as I contemplate the draconian anti-crime bill which is now before the General Assembly. Most appalling is the plank that would give police the power to seize DNA samples from anyone arrested for a crime, be it shoplifting or murder. This is a monstrous invasion of privacy and violation of the Fourth Amendment. South Carolina's proposed DNA-gathering law would be the most aggressive in the nation and surely land the state in a swamp of litigation.

Legislators are "pretending to be tough on crime and playing the fear card," an ACLU spokesman said. "Stripping people of their rights, that's not the place to start. Trying to create a police state, that's not the place to start."

Yet my bet is that the vast majority of South Carolinians support this bill, including the ferocious freedom fighters who stormed Charleston City Council last month to demand their god-given right to smoke in public places.

What a strange state we live in.

February 7, 2007

(The General Assembly passed a version of this legislation in 2008, then overrode Gov. Mark Sanford's veto.)

THE LAST LYNCHING
SIXTY YEARS LATER, WILLIE EARLE STILL HAUNTS US

Strom Thurmond had been at home in the governor's mansion less than a month when the phone rang early on the morning of February 17, 1947, with the chilling news.

There had been a lynching in Pickens County. A 24-year-old black man named Willie Earle had been seized from the county jail by a mob, carried across the Greenville County line and beaten, stabbed, and blasted twice at close range with a shotgun.

There was no secret who the murderers were. A Greenville taxi driver named Thomas Watson Brown had been robbed and fatally stabbed in Pickens County on February 15. Piecing together circumstantial evidence, authorities arrested Earle at his mother's house the next day. That night, Greenville taxi drivers organized a convoy of cabs, drove to the Pickens County jail, demanded the prisoner, and murdered him.

The Willie Earle lynching was a horrible embarrassment to a state which sought to recast its image as a civilized, progressive province, suitable for investment and development. And it was an early challenge for Strom Thurmond, who —at that stage in his career—had cast himself as a racial moderate.

"I do not favor lynching and I shall exert every resource at my command to apprehend all persons who may be involved in such a flagrant violation of the law," the governor declared in dispatching a state constable to Greenville County.

Within hours of the lynching, the U.S. Marshal's Service and the FBI were involved in the investigation. Over the next four days, over 150 suspects were questioned before authorities charged 31 men --28 of them taxi drivers, all of them white. Most of the men signed confessions; several of their statements identified Roosevelt Carlos Hurd as the leader of the mob and the man who killed Earle with the shotgun.

Over the next weeks, *Time* and *Newsweek* magazines praised

Thurmond's decisive action against racial violence. Newspapers in Greenville and around the South condemned lynching. But in markets and restaurants throughout the Upstate, white businesses put out jars to collect money for the legal defense of the taxi drivers.

The eyes of the nation and the world were on the Greenville County Courthouse as the lynching trial opened on May 5, 1947. *The New Yorker* sent Dame Rebecca West to cover the trial. *Life* magazine had a reporter and photographer in the courtroom and ran a major photo spread of the proceedings. Wire services carried the story from coast to coast and in Europe. Reporters from Northern black newspapers were allowed into the packed and sweltering courtroom, but were forced to sit in the upper gallery.

Relying on a quaint eccentricity of state law, wives and children of the 31 defendants sat with their men in the front of the courtroom, attempting to demonstrate their wholesome, stalwart nature. West wrote that the arrangement gave the proceedings the atmosphere of a church picnic.

Throughout the two-week trial, defense attorneys pandered to the basest prejudices and fears of the jury. At one point, an attorney announced to the jury, "Willie Earle is dead and I wish more like him was dead."

Wrote West: "There was a delighted giggling, almost coquettish response from the defendants and some of the spectators ... A more disgusting incident could not have happened in any court of law at any time."

One cab driver who had refused to go along with the lynch party was called by the state to identify some of the men who did. He was later beaten and forced to leave town.

The prosecution rested and the defense refused to call any witnesses. On the afternoon of May 21, Judge J. Robert Martin gave his charge to the jury. Five hours and thirteen minutes later, the 12 good men and true had reached their verdicts: not guilty on all counts.

Pandemonium broke out on the floor of the courtroom after the verdicts were read; in the gallery above, there was stunned silence.

When order was restored, Judge Martin, shaken and angry,

informed the jury where they could pick up their fees for service. Then he stood, turned his back on the jury and left the courtroom without the customary courtesy of thanking them for their service.

Willie Earle's was the last lynching in South Carolina, but hardly the last lynching in the South. James Ford Seale was arrested last month in the 1964 kidnapping and murder of two black youths in Mississippi. In recent years, authorities have won convictions in the 1963 assassination of NAACP activist Medgar Evers; the 1963 Birmingham, Ala., church bombing that killed four black girls; and the 1964 Philadelphia, Miss., slayings of three civil rights workers. But the murderers of Willie Earle will never be punished. They had their day in court and the jury found that killing a black man in South Carolina was not a crime.

February 14, 2007

BLOOD ON THE STREETS
VIOLENCE FUELS CHARLESTON'S RACIAL DIVIDE

Gunshots rang out a few doors from my apartment one night recently. Five of them. Or maybe six. I am culturally and temperamentally indisposed to count gunshots.

What made these shots so unusual was that they were early in the evening — about 10:30. The shootings which have plagued so much of the Charleston urban environment in recent months usually occur between 1 and 5 a.m. I am usually asleep during much of this period, but I read the names and details in the paper a couple of days after the fact.

The second unusual thing about this incident is that there were no bodies. The police swarmed through the neighborhood, knocked on doors, stopped pedestrians, and asked anyone they could find what they knew. When it was over, there was nothing to report — no bodies, no charges, no arrests.

I wish it always ended so innocuously. The first notice that I had crossed a divide, that I had entered a new culture and a new phase of my life occurred on an August night in 2002, about four months after I moved to Charleston.

Walking home from a local tavern, I approached the intersection of Rutledge Avenue and Sumter Street, which was cordoned off. Blue lights flashed as an anxious crowd gathered in the sultry night. It was the night 13-year-old Velvet Brown died, gunned down in a drive-by shooting. Looking up Sumter Street, I could make out the covered form of her body on the pavement, more than an hour after she was killed.

A few days later, 23-year-old Earl Allen was charged with the murder, after he had been named by four eyewitnesses as the shooter. But when the case came to trial 15 months later, the witnesses had recanted their statements and the prosecution was forced to drop the charges. No one has been tried for Velvet Brown's murder.

The death of this 13-year-old sparked weeks of soul-searching in the community. There were speeches and sermons and pledges that we would get to the bottom of this, we would root out the problem of violence in the community. We are still praying, talking, and wishing.

Of course, the vast majority of the murders in the Charleston area are black-on-black crimes. To most white residents, reading about the wave of black murder victims is like reading the news from Darfur or some other exotic killing field. It doesn't happen to them. Street crime is one more cultural wedge that is driving blacks and whites apart in Charleston County and throughout the nation.

But this is not social theory to the people whose sons and daughters are dying on the streets in senseless feuds, turf wars, and drug deals. Prayer has carried African Americans through some terrible times in the past. It remains to be seen whether it will deliver them from this plague of self-imposed carnage.

There was a "rally against violence" downtown last autumn. The 500 block of King Street was closed to traffic while rappers and blues singers performed, community leaders spoke and prayed, vendors sold food and CDs. A month later, at 3 a.m. on November 12, Graylin Milligan was killed in a hail of bullets in front of LJ's Soul Food Cafe, on the very spot where the rally had been held. Milligan's death broke Charleston's record of 20 murders, set in 1969.

It seems to be a season for irony. Two weeks ago, politicians and preachers gathered at Nichols Chapel AME Church, to plan another rally against violence. The church stands at the intersection of President and Bogard streets, where Terri Lynn Melendez was shot to death on March 15. And the good citizens of North Charleston rallied and prayed against violence on Saturday, May 26. At 2:30 a.m., 36 hours later and a few blocks away, 21-year-old Harri Singleton died of multiple gunshot wounds.

As for Earl Allen, he died at 2 a.m. on the morning of June 4, 2006, near the corner of Rutledge Avenue and Strawberry Lane, six blocks from the place Velvet Brown died four years before. The man who killed him was awaiting trial on another murder charge.

For blacks, the answer to this bloodshed is more prayer, more rallies. For whites, it is escape.

I was on Daniel Island for the first time two weeks ago and was shocked by the sterility, the blandness, the whiteness of the place. But one thing you've got to say for Daniel Island — there are no street killings and every time one punk dispatches another somewhere in Charleston County, Daniel Island becomes a little more appealing to white families who just want to live in peace. And the racial divide in Charleston grows a little wider. That is the other tragedy in the body count on Charleston's streets.

June 6, 2007

COMING TO TERMS WITH TILLMAN
WHAT ARE WE TO DO WITH PITCHFORK BEN?

Some years ago, when I was living in downtown Columbia, I would take late-night walks down Main Street to the Statehouse on warm spring or summer nights.

On the vast grounds around that impressive granite capitol, I could walk in reflective silence among the trees and statuary. The monument to the Confederate soldier was here, as well as the monument to Confederate women. There was the monument to Gen. Wade Hampton, sitting upon his great anatomically correct steed, and the more modest bronze image of James F. Byrnes, sitting in judicial robes, a book of law open across his lap.

And there was the other statue which haunted those silent grounds and haunted my conscience. Benjamin Ryan Tillman stood there, larger than life, on a stone pedestal, near the front entrance to the Statehouse. Just stood there in his great bronze overcoat, arms by his sides, fists clenched, glowering down at the world.

That's pretty much the way he went through life, actually. He was an angry, violent man in an angry, violent time, and he rode those emotions to fame and power and a place on the Statehouse lawn.

Tillman was a paramilitary fighter who waged war on the biracial, federally supported state government of Reconstruction. He was present at the Hamburg Massacre of 1876, where black activists were captured and murdered by the "Redshirts." The Reconstruction government collapsed later that year.

Ben Tillman was an ambitious and instinctive politician who hijacked the state Farmers Alliance and rode it to the Governor's Mansion in 1890. As champion of the common man — meaning, of course, the common white man — he was instrumental in the creation of Clemson College and Winthrop College (now universities), as alternatives to the more elite College of South Carolina (now USC) and The Citadel. (He called The Citadel a "dude factory.") He was elected to the U.S. Senate in 1894 and served until his death in 1918.

Throughout his long political career, he was an outspoken white supremacist who used his considerable oratorical gifts to rouse white resentment against black people. He organized the state constitutional convention of 1895, which disenfranchised blacks and led to the segregation laws which stood for 70 years.

Tillman was remarkably honest about his means and his ends. On one occasion he proclaimed, "We of the South have never recognized the right of the Negro to govern white men, and we never will. We have never believed him to be the equal of the white man, and we will not submit to his gratifying his lust on our wives and daughters without lynching him."

Another time he said, "We have done our level best [to disenfranchise blacks] ...We stuffed ballot boxes. We shot them. We are not ashamed of it."

This is the man who has welcomed visitors up the concourse to the front of the Statehouse since 1940. I used to fantasize about backing a pickup truck onto the grounds, tossing a rope around Tillman's neck and yanking him off that pedestal. On a quiet summer night in those pre-9/11 days, I could have probably done it and gotten away. Now that may not be necessary.

Rep. Todd Rutherford (D-Richland) has introduced a resolution to remove the statue from the Statehouse grounds. In a counter measure, Columbia Mayor Bob Coble (another Democrat) has proposed putting a plaque on Tillman's pedestal which would give a more balanced assessment of the politician's legacy.

College of Charleston historian Jack Bass favors the second measure.

It's a "complicated" issue, Bass said in a telephone interview, and Tillman was a "complicated" figure.

"Without question, Ben Tillman was a racist," Bass said, but he only reflected the views of the vast majority of Southern whites at the time. When he wasn't on the stump, Tillman actually spoke and worked quietly against lynching. And, the professor added, Tillman was willing to work with blacks when it was necessary.

Tillman is "a significant historic figure in South Carolina," Bass said. "To remove that statue is to obscure that part of our history."

Perhaps, but I don't buy it. The facts Bass cites do not atone for the damage Tillman did to a large number of people and to the democratic process in South Carolina. I think it's time to take the old demagogue down from his pedestal and pack him off to some museum. That's what museums are for — to serve as repositories for those ideas and objects we no longer use or cherish, but whose historic or cultural significance we recognize.

I think that's a fair description of Ben Tillman in the twenty-first century. He should be remembered, not enshrined.

January 20, 2008

(Rutherford's resolution did not make it out of committee. See www.downwithtillman.com)

POISON POLITICS
S.C. INFECTS THE AMERICAN BODY POLITIC

I have written about it before — the venom that South Carolina has historically injected into the nation's political blood stream.

Let's recount: South Carolina led the march to secession in 1860 and launched the country on four years of internecine slaughter. Since then, its politicians — men such as "Pitchfork Ben" Tillman, "Cotton Ed" Smith, and Strom Thurmond — have spewed their racist vitriol in the national forum. Throughout the 1990s, the battle over the Confederate flag above the Statehouse mesmerized the nation and turned the state capitol into a rallying point for white supremacists.

Early in the 2000 presidential campaign, the Republican train moved from the Iowa caucuses to the New Hampshire primaries and into the Palmetto State. Along the way Sen. John McCain defeated Texas Gov. George W. Bush in Iowa and routed him in New Hampshire. One more defeat and Bush would have been on his way back to Austin.

But in South Carolina, a mysterious — and now legendary — smear campaign of last-minute phone calls and fliers made sure that wouldn't happen. Potential GOP voters were told, among other things, that McCain's wife was a prescription drug addict and that the senator was the father of an illegitimate black girl. Both charges were untrue — and the second, too ironic to have happened anywhere except South Carolina. But enough white voters believed it. More importantly, they were sufficiently outraged to go forth and give the primary to Bush and launch him on his way to the White House. It can be argued that all the corruption, malfeasance, diplomatic wreckage, and fiscal mismanagement wrought by this administration can be laid at the feet of Palmetto State Republicans.

Now our perverted values have once again poisoned the well of national politics.

Coming into the Democratic primary last week, Barack Obama was heralded as a new kind of politician. His caucus victory in overwhelmingly white Iowa seemed to prove that he transcended racial politics. By uniting blacks and whites, he would show the way to a new post-racial America.

Then he hit the Palmetto Jungle, where nothing is without racial tint.

Politics being what they are in this state, the vast majority of white people vote in the Republican primary and an even larger majority of blacks vote in the Democratic primary. (Approximately 55 percent of Democratic voters on January 26 were black.)

In the months leading up to that primary, polls showed Obama and Hillary Clinton running neck-and-neck to capture the state's black vote. Indeed, a number of the state's black political leaders — including Sen. Robert Ford of Charleston — had endorsed Clinton.

And why not? Bill and Hillary Clinton are long-time civil rights champions. The empathy between black folk and the poor white boy from Arkansas is legendary. Toni Morrison boldly declared Bill Clinton to be "America's first black president."

Whether Bill Clinton was a loose cannon or was taking orders from his wife's campaign in the week before the primary is still not clear. What is clear is that somebody felt that desperate measures were called for in this critical state.

Bill Clinton uncorked the racial rhetoric, saying that he feared his wife could not win in South Carolina because Democrats would be voting on racial identity. On another occasion he compared Obama to black activist Jesse Jackson, who ran for president in 1984 and 1988. In those years Jackson made good showings in the South Carolina Democratic primary, but did not come close to winning the nomination. It was a thinly veiled reminder that a black candidate was unelectable.

By most accounts, Clinton's rhetoric backfired. Obama defeated Hillary Clinton 55 percent to 27 percent. But exit polls show that while he carried nearly 80 percent of the black vote, he got only 25 percent of the white vote.

The damage done in South Carolina was extensive. Barack Obama was "racialized." He came out of the state looking like the "official black candidate."

Will he be able to shake that image down the stretch to the August convention? He is still a long shot to win the nomination, and the odds of victory are even slimmer in the general election if he is branded the "black candidate."

And what about Bill Clinton and his legacy as a racial moderate? That legacy took a hit in South Carolina, as did his reputation as a brilliantly instinctive politician. Not only did he alienate black voters and cause his wife to lose by a landslide, but he left the state with a new reputation — the man who played the race card. I'm betting his wife's campaign will recover from this disaster before his image does.

Such is the power of South Carolina to racialize politics and bring out the worst in good people. It's a curse we bear and we impart to the nation and we seem unable to exorcise it.

February 6, 2008

(Of course, Bill Clinton's reputation survived the campaign; his wife did not. And Barack Obama went on to the White House.)

REDISCOVERING BLACK HISTORY
IT'S ALWAYS BEEN HERE; IT'S JUST BEEN BURIED

History, like theology, inspires the passions and genius of some, the scorn and ridicule of others. Also like theology, history is never concluded. It periodically must be re-imagined, reconstructed, and rewritten to keep it fresh and relevant.

Anyone who thinks that history and theology are closed books clearly understands neither. Modern Christians are embarrassed by their nineteenth-century white southern counterparts who justified the institution of slavery with chapter and verse from the Bible. White Southerners had to rationalize the peculiar institution; their society and economy were built on it.

White Southerners have also rationalized a lot of history over the centuries. Anyone raised in South Carolina a few decades ago was exposed to the history books of Mary C. Simms Oliphant. This little woman — the granddaughter of poet and southern apologist William Gilmore Simms — held the franchise on the South Carolina history textbooks used in state public schools from the 1920s to the 1980s.

In her books, Oliphant managed to recount the story of South Carolina from 1670 to the time of Strom Thurmond with barely a mention of black people or slavery. In a state that was built on the labor of African Americans, a state whose politics and culture have been defined by the need to control the black population, Oliphant managed to reduce that population to a handful of references.

But sometimes change has to come — even in South Carolina.

"You can almost feel something bubbling under the surface," Simon Lewis said in an interview last week. Lewis is director of the Program in Carolina Lowcountry and Atlantic World (CLAW), and his antennae are more sensitive than most.

CLAW is a group of scholars seeking to rediscover the Charleston of the seventeenth and eighteenth centuries before it was redefined by southern politics and regionalism. They are also trying to rediscover the role of black people in this city at a time when they were the majority and connected to the wider world by commerce and culture.

Charleston 200 years ago was a great spoke in the wheel of Atlantic commerce that reached from Northeastern port cities to Europe, Africa, and the Caribbean, Lewis said. It was a cosmopolitan and multinational city, looking outward to the wider world. One of its chief imports was African slaves. It is estimated that 40 percent of all slaves brought into the United States came through the port of Charleston.

The rise of the abolitionist movement — in Britain and the northern U.S. — began to alter Charleston's place in the world and the place of black people in Charleston, Lewis said. Faced with increasingly hostile attitudes toward slavery, Charleston began to withdraw from the wider world; it began to look inward. The city's role in the opening of the Civil War cemented its place as a quintessentially "southern" city. It remained southern and provincial until recent decades when it once again emerged as an important international port.

At the same time Charleston was redefining itself, it was redefining black people. White people's fear of abolition led to the ideology of racism and the "science" of racism in an effort to justify slavery. Lewis quoted cultural historian Nancy Stepan: "As the battle for abolition was being won, the battle against racism was being lost."

The ideology of racism — which permeated every niche and crevice of white society — effectively dehumanized black people. Not only were they stripped of all legal rights and protections, they were effectively written out of history. This "whites only" view of history is what generations of Southerners — black and white — have been taught in public schools and public celebrations.

But today that is changing. Lewis sees the changes in many ways, large and small. He sees it in the ceremony two weeks ago to dedicate the new African American Cemetery Memorial on the College of Charleston campus. He sees it in the comment in Gov. Mark Sanford's recent State of the State address that it is time for South Carolinians to come to terms with the past. He sees it in the recent biracial family reunion at historic Drayton Hall plantation and in the opening of the Old Slave Mart Museum downtown.

There are a hundred aphorisms and epigrams to define history. I like Edmund Burke's: "History is a pact between the dead, the living and the yet unborn."

It is our responsibility to be faithful to one another and to that pact. We can do that only by keeping our minds and hearts open to the possibilities and by understanding that the final word will never be written.

February 20, 2008

CAVE DWELLERS
FEAR WILL BE THE DECIDER FOR MANY WHITES ON ELECTION DAY

At the end of World War II, there were thousands of Japanese soldiers abandoned by their retreating comrades across China, Southeast Asia, and the islands of the South Pacific. In many cases, they had no radios or other means of communicating with the outside world; no way of knowing that the war was over, or how it ended. Mainland troops were rounded up quickly enough, but things were different on the remote islands.

Over the next years these Robinson Crusoes began to emerge from their caves and jungle hideouts, surrendering to whomever was available. They would end their isolation, even if it meant becoming prisoners of the dreaded Americans. Their "captors" were invariably shocked at the ragged, bearded ghosts who straggled out of the jungle, hands held high, blinking in the sunlight.

Needless to say, most of these unreconstructed warriors of the Rising Sun found things had changed dramatically since they left home. There were now televisions and transistor radios; the emperor was no longer god; an elected parliament ran the country. Perhaps most shocking was the fact the United States — the devil they had sacrificed so many years to defeat — was now a friend and ally. The last and most famous Japanese holdout was Lt. Hiroo Onada. In 1974, Onada was talked out of his hiding place on a remote Philippine island by his former commanding officer.

Onada later wrote of that meeting with his commander in the jungle: "Suddenly everything went black. A storm raged inside me. I felt like a fool for having been so tense and cautious on the way here [to meet his commander]. Worse than that, what had I been doing for all these years?

"Gradually the storm subsided, and for the first time I really understood: my 30 years as a guerrilla fighter for the Japanese army were abruptly finished. This was the end.

"I pulled back the bolt on my rifle and unloaded the bullets ... I eased off the pack that I always carried with me and laid the gun on top of it. Would I really have no more use for this rifle that I had polished and cared for like a baby all these years? ... Had the war really ended 30 years ago? ... If what was happening was true, wouldn't it have been better if I had died with [my comrades]?"

I think of those Japanese soldiers sometimes when I consider the white Southerners who are still fighting the Civil War in their hearts. Of course, they would deny this. But on Election Day, most white Southerners will line up with the Republican Party, as they have since 1964, the year the Democrats passed the Civil Rights Act. They still hide in their cave of white solidarity, unable to imagine a world that is not divided along racial lines.

On Election Day, millions of white people of different ethnicities, regions, classes, ambitions, and education levels, will be united by the one thing that is more powerful than any of these others — their white skin. And their white fear.

But in this election, more white Southerners will be voting Democratic than at any time in recent history, and they will do it for one reason: Barack Obama.

Obama is a transformational figure, who is showing people — especially young people — the way to a post-racial society. What we will see on Tuesday is a record number of white Southerners voting out of hope, rather than voting out of fear.

In South Carolina, there is even giddy talk that Obama might carry this backward and benighted little state. In *The Post and Courier* last week, Sixth District Rep. Jim Clyburn said, "I think it is a long shot, but it is not as long a shot today as it was a month ago."

Perhaps, but polls show Republican John McCain with a 20-point lead in South Carolina, the typical margin between Republicans and Democrats in presidential races in our state, 12 days before the election. Still, I think this election might be closer than the pollsters predict, because Obama has electrified the young people in this state, and this is a demographic that lives by the cell phone and has no land lines. They could not be reached by pollsters. Their voices will be heard only on Election Day. In some states, they are going to be Obama's margin of victory. In the Palmetto State, I think, they will be the margin of surprise.

Regardless of the final vote, this election brings us closer to the day when white South Carolinians can come out of their cave of fear and understand the war is really over.

October 29, 2008

INSTITUTIONAL BIGOTRY
CAN CHRISTIAN CONSERVATIVES LEARN FROM THEIR SINS?

Confession, they say, is good for the soul, and we have had two important confessions recently. Perhaps it is the election of a black man as president of the United States, but more likely it was years of soul-searching and introspection — the kind I like to think many Americans have been doing since November 4 — which caused two hidebound institutions to come forward and apologize for their racist pasts.

You probably heard that Bob Jones University, the private, fundamentalist Christian school in Greenville, issued a statement two weeks ago acknowledging "institutional policies regarding race" which had influenced its attitudes and behavior for half a century. Specifically, BJU did not accept black students until 1971, and its policy against interracial dating was not lifted until nine years ago.

"We failed to accurately represent the Lord and to fulfill the commandment to love others as ourselves," the university declared on its website on Noember. 20. "For these failures we are profoundly sorry."

The BJU statement comes months after the American Medical Association offered a similar mea culpa. From its founding in 1847, until recent decades, the AMA had denied membership to black physicians. More recently, when it did begin to accept minority individuals, it refused to take action against local medical associations which continued to discriminate.

In the July 16 issue of the *Journal of the American Medical Association*, Ronald M. Davis wrote that many of the organization's questionable actions reflected the "social mores and racial discrimination" that existed for much of the country's history. But, he wrote, that should not excuse such behavior.

These recent apologies come after more than a decade of contrition from other public and private institutions. These have included the states of Alabama, Maryland, North Carolina, New Jersey, Virginia, and Florida and businesses such as Wachovia, which have expressed regret for their roles in slavery. Last year, the governing board of the University of Virginia passed a resolution of "regret for its use of enslaved persons from 1819 to 1865."

In 1997, President Bill Clinton expressed regret for the "Tuskegee experiment," in which U.S. government researchers used black men to study syphilis without their knowledge of consent. Starting in 1932, researchers treating almost 400 men infected with syphilis gave them placebos and then observed the progression of the disease. The study continued until 1972, when its existence was leaked to the media. Clinton called the study "deeply, profoundly, morally wrong."

In 2005, the Republican Party apologized for its racially tinged "Southern Strategy," which it adopted during Richard Nixon's 1968 campaign.

And there was the 1995 apology of the Southern Baptist Convention for its long history of racism. As part of its 150th anniversary observance, the SBC issued a resolution acknowledging that it was created in 1845 in a schism among American Baptists over the issue of southern slavery. The resolution marked the denomination's first formal acknowledgment that racism played a role in its founding.

The resolution acknowledged that because of the SBC's links to slavery, "our relationship to African-Americans has been hindered from the beginning," and that more recently Southern Baptists "failed in many cases to support and in some cases opposed legitimate initiatives to secure the civil rights of African-Americans."

Yes, a confession is good for the soul, but is an apology sincere if one has not had a change of heart, if one has not learned from past mistakes? I direct this question specifically at Bob Jones University and the Southern Baptist Convention, two deeply conservative religious institutions which influence local politics and culture, yet seem particularly incapable of learning from the past.

The SBC continues to stand by past resolutions rejecting homosexuality as a "lifestyle" and referring to it as a "manifestation of a depraved nature," "a perversion of divine standards and as a violation of nature and natural affections," and "an abomination in the eyes of God." More specifically, it denies full citizenship to homosexuals by opposing same-sex marriages and equivalent unions.

Likewise, BJU's stance on homosexuality is uncompromising. It not only kicked Starbucks off campus because it was seen as "gay-friendly," it threatens its own gay alumni with arrest if they come onto campus. Last year three gay rights activists were arrested for entering the campus.

In justifying their intolerance, both BJU and the SBC cite the same Bible they quoted for generations to defend slavery and segregation. They were just as righteous and intransigent then as they are today. But I would bet — and I will not be around to collect on this one — that in about 40 years when all the gay rights battles have been won and society has moved on to other issues, BJU and the SBC will offer a meek and irrelevant apology for the hateful things they are saying and doing today.

December 3, 2008

TALKING RACISM
AND WE'RE GOING TO KEEP TALKING UNTIL IT GOES AWAY

Last spring I was driving west on Calhoun Street with my Obama stickers from last year still proudly displayed on my rear bumper. An old Chevrolet pickup truck roared by me and up the James Island Connector ramp. As it passed, some yahoo shouted from the passenger seat, "Obama sucks!"

Was that political commentary or racist diatribe?

A lot of people have been asking themselves that question lately in the wake of months of rowdy town hall meetings where people have carried posters depicting the president as Hitler; at one Obama appearance, one man brought a gun. And, of course, there was Rep. Joe Wilson (R-S.C.) with his shout of "You lie!" at President Obama during a speech to a joint session of Congress.

All in all, it's been an ugly summer in America. But what made it ugly? Partisan politics or sublimated racism?

The summer is finally over. Congress has reconvened. The pundits have found other things to yammer about. Right now a lot of people are breathing a deep sigh of relief. Well, you can suck that sigh back in. I'm here to stir the pot, fan the flames, kick the hornet nest — choose your metaphor.

I want to talk about racism in America. It's a national conversation we have needed for a long time. I agree with Bill Maher, who said recently, "Finally, we're talking about this."

Damn straight. Let's keep talking.

Racism is the elephant in America's living room. We can refuse to talk about it, or we may speak loftily of living in a post-elephant home. But the beast still stinks and poops on the floor and knocks over the furniture. And sometimes it gets angry and smashes the whole house. We ignore it at our own peril.

Following Wilson's outburst, there was much commentary and condemnation. It all broke down along predictable party and ideological lines, starting with former President Jimmy Carter, who told CNN, "I think it's based on racism. There is an inherent feeling among many in this country that an African-American should not be president ... Those kind of things are not just casual outcomes of a sincere debate on whether we should have a national program on healthcare. It's deeper than that."

New York Times columnist Maureen Dowd wrote: "Wilson's shocking disrespect for the office of president ... convinced me: Some people just can't believe a black man is president and will never accept it."

Conservative columnist Cal Thomas denied any taint of racism with a typically asinine offering: "Obama supporters will have difficulty explaining how a mostly white country could elect a black man president last November and 10 months later become a racist majority."

Actually, Cal, nobody said there was a racist majority in this country. Among the 46 percent of voters who cast their ballots for John McCain in November, I am sure there were many —

perhaps a majority — whose reasons were purely political. But common sense dictates that there were many others with darker motives. Anyone who saw the videos of Sarah Palin's rallies last fall could not mistake the inarticulate rage of some of those people for a policy discussion. And healthcare wasn't even under discussion back then.

My friend and colleague Jack Hunter wrote that "for many liberals, the proof [of racism] is circumstantial." Perhaps it is, Jack, but many malefactors have been convicted on circumstantial evidence. And there are generations of it to choose from.

Bigots have a long history of sublimating their poison with lofty, high-sounding motives. When Gov. Strom Thurmond addressed the Dixiecrat convention and accepted its presidential nomination in 1948, he told the hall full of howling racists, "I want to tell you, ladies and gentlemen, that there's not enough troops in the Army to force the Southern people to break down segregation and admit the Negro race into our theaters, into our swimming pools, into our homes, and into our churches."

Of course, when he stepped out of the hall and into the bright lights of the media and the larger world, he spoke in terms of "states' rights" and constitutional principles. How many of the bigots of 2009 are hiding behind the rhetoric of healthcare?

Whether or not the most extreme anti-Obama behavior is motivated by racism or by a deep and genuine fear of a public option healthcare plan, the important thing is that we talk about it. Racism is alive in America — maybe it's not doing as well as it was a few decades ago, but it's always looking for a comeback and another opening in our civic armor. Failure to acknowledge this is not just dishonest — it is dangerous.

Let's keep talking about racism.

September 30, 2009

CONFUSED WHITE PEOPLE
ON AUGUST 28, IGNORANCE LOOKED PRETTY BLISSFUL

I have lived long enough to witness some important changes in American culture and the way Americans think, behave, and speak.

When I was growing up in South Carolina a half-century ago, every white person I knew was a segregationist and a racist to a greater or lesser degree. And if there were any white people who did not share those views, they were smart enough to keep it to themselves.

It is a tribute to the humanity of the civil rights movement and the basic decency of the American people that so much has changed — even in the South. One of those changes has been in the way Americans use language. The "N-word," as it has come to be known, is now verboten. Its use can cost a person his social standing or her job, as it did with a right-wing radio personality recently.

Likewise, the word "racist" itself has been transformed. Fifty years ago, racist speech and behavior were perfectly respectable, even *de rigueur*. Whites not demonstrating sufficient hostility to blacks and suspicion of the civil rights movement might be ostracized — or worse.

Today "racist" is one of the strongest pejoratives in the language. No one — not even a racist — can allow the word to be hung on him. It is almost comic to watch conservative politicians backtrack and stumble over themselves (as several South Carolina pols have done in the last couple of years), trying to explain that their racist remarks were misunderstood, were taken out of context, were meant in jest.

I realized the language had undergone a strange mutation a couple of years ago when I observed that my critics had begun calling me a racist in their responses to my columns and blogs. Presumably, they were angry at my criticism of white people for their historic bigotry, their subsequent distortion of history, and their glorification of violence and folly. And presumably, they took my motivation for writing such things to be racism against white people, ignoring the fact that I am white, my family is white, and the majority of my friends and associates are white.

So what does "racism" mean in the twenty-first century? Is it just the pejorative of last resort for those of limited vocabulary? Did the civil rights movement so effectively stigmatize the behavior that even racists find the tag a handy cudgel against their adversaries?

And what does "honor" mean today? What does it mean in the mouth of a man like Glenn Beck?

I've wondered about Beck's state of mind in the past as I watched the tears stream down his face on his Fox News show. He reminds me of Tammy Faye Bakker, who used to open the faucets and streak her mascara while fleecing the lambs with her husband Jim at her side on PTL.

A few months ago, when Beck announced that he would hold a rally at the Lincoln Memorial, on the 47th anniversary of Martin Luther King Jr.'s "I Have A Dream" speech, there was appropriate outrage and consternation. The reaction was because Beck had so clearly taken that great moment in American history and turned it on its head.

"We were the people that did it in the first place," Beck announced last spring on Fox News.

Did what in the first place? Stood up to ignorance, bigotry, and violence? No, Beck and his Fox News colleagues have never done that. They have fanned ignorance, bigotry, and violence with their Islamophobia and homophobia. And instinctively one knows that if Beck and Fox had been around in 1963, they would have been railing against Martin Luther King Jr. and everything he stood for.

"This is a moment, quite honestly, that I think we reclaim the civil rights movement," Beck proclaimed with no sense of irony. "It has been so distorted and so turned upside down because we must repair honor and integrity first ... We will take that movement because we were the people that did it in the first place."

And so a hundred thousand white people gathered at the Lincoln Memorial on Aug. 28 for Beck's Restoring Honor rally, another linguistic contortion that failed to address whose honor was being restored and how it was lost.

"Political language," George Orwell wrote, "is designed to make lies sound truthful and murder respectable and to give an appearance of solidity to pure wind."

There was much wind and lying at the Lincoln Memorial on Aug. 28, and it all sounded very respectable. Such is the power of language when people no longer care or remember what words mean.

September 8, 2010

REMEMBERING THE OTHER CIVIL WAR
THAT WOULD BE THE ONE WE ARE STILL FIGHTING

When America began the observance of the Civil War centennial, we were a very different country from what we are today. In 1961, we had not lost a war in Vietnam. We had not seen a wave of our leaders assassinated. We were only beginning to experience the transforming power of communication technology. And we were still a racially segregated society that was barely different from what it had been in the late nineteenth century.

We were an innocent and optimistic people in 1961. For most Americans, the centennial was the celebration of America reunited. In the great morality play that was our Civil War centennial, there were no villains, unless you counted John Wilkes Booth, but he was not really a soldier and he wasn't really in the war. Americans 50 years ago knew the Civil War as a series of romanticized vignettes of Johnny Reb and Billy Yank, those brave and honorable cavaliers who fought a tragic war over ... well, there wasn't much discussion of what the war was about. That wasn't important in 1961.

What was important was that it was over, that we were all Americans, that the United States had emerged from that inferno to become a global superpower, that we had won two world wars and made the world safe for democracy, that we were the shining city on the hill, the torch of freedom, the last, best hope for mankind — pick your cliché. And it all happened because we had passed some great test of fire one hundred years before. It didn't quite make sense to my 11-year-old mind in 1961, but like most of my South Carolina upbringing, I didn't question it.

America has grown up a lot in 50 years. We've had our hearts broken and our faith tested. We've endured some dark nights of the soul. We find ourselves a more complex nation, living in a more complex world than ever before. Maybe now it is safe to see our Civil War for what it truly was. Yes, it was a war between North and South, but it was more. It was a war between white and black, between slave and slave owner.

These were facts that a younger America was not ready to face 50 years ago, especially in the South, as the civil rights movement began to gather momentum. And because white Southerners refused to talk about it, white Northerners politely acquiesced. And so the great issue behind the great war was never seriously discussed in any way that I remember during the Civil War centennial. The little war within the big war was not acknowledged.

There was no recounting of the slave Robert Smalls, who hijacked a Confederate steamer in Charleston Harbor and turned it over to the Union Navy waiting beyond Fort Sumter. There was no mention of the valiant attack of the black troops of the Massachusetts 54th Regiment against Battery Wagner on Morris Island. There was no talk of the thousands of freed slaves in the Port Royal area who enlisted in the Union Army. Indeed, there was no discussion at all of the 200,000 black troops in the Union Army. And the Emancipation Proclamation was a curious footnote in this great epic of blood and glory, of brother against brother.

In this sense, the centennial observance of the Civil War was much like the half-century observance. That, too, was a celebration of America reunited, and for that occasion D.W. Griffith unveiled his cinematic masterpiece, *Birth of a Nation*. This early silent film is remembered today for its highly racist perspective and glorification of the Ku Klux Klan. But in 1915, *Birth of a Nation* was seen as a tribute to the new nation born, as its title suggests, out of the Civil War and Reconstruction. The homily of the movie is the reunification of the nation, as symbolized in the closing scene by the weddings of the Northern Stoneman siblings to the Southern Camerons. But before the joyous nuptials could occur, the families had to stand fast against the scourge of black Reconstruction. Or, as one subtitle puts it: "The former enemies of North and South are united again in defense of their Aryan birthright."

Yes, *Birth of a Nation* was produced as an idealized tribute to a new America, not completely unlike the new America that we celebrated in 1961. Today, the question is whether we have grown up enough to see our history more accurately and fairly. Will we continue to hide from our past? Are we ready to face that other civil war, the one that still divides us, the one that we read about in our newspapers every day? Will that war ever be over?

We will know it's over when we stop denying that it ever happened.

April 6. 2011

THE DEBATE THAT NEVER ENDS
BY 2061, WILL WE KNOW WHAT CAUSED THE CIVIL WAR?

On Tuesday, we heard the first shots of the Civil War re-enacted at Fort Sumter, 150 years after the real shots that inspired them. At first blush, it would seem that all is peace, nostalgia, and remembrance in the sesquicentennial of America's bloodiest war.

But if the letters to the editors in our state's newspapers are any indication, there is at least one issue that is still hotly contested and widely misunderstood. That, of course, is the cause of the secession and war.

I will not belabor the point here, as anyone capable of reading is capable of learning the truth. The Southern states — including South Carolina — declared very clearly and directly in their secession documents that their purpose was to defend slavery against Northern, abolitionist, and Republican imperatives.

In 1861, Alexander Stephens, vice president of the Confederacy, declared, "Our new government['s] ... foundations are laid, its cornerstone rests, upon the great truth that the negro is not equal to the white man; that slavery — subordination to the superior race — is his natural and moral condition."

It is all there in black and white. The founders of the Confederacy did not mince words.

But I was surprised at one name I found last week among the neo-secessionists and historical revisionists on the editorial and op-ed pages: Kirkpatrick Sale.

A former Vermont resident, Sale is one of America's most interesting — and perhaps most important — public intellectuals. He has written a number of books, including a history of the Students for a Democratic Society and *Conquest of Paradise: Christopher Columbus and the Columbian Legacy*, a refreshingly different interpretation of the great explorer. But what he is most noted for in recent years is his critique of technology and its impact on human beings and the environment. Machines and capital have led to the creation of enormous corporations and empires, he writes, designed to control people and resources for the purpose of creating profit.

Sale's solution to this crisis is to create smaller states by breaking up the huge nations that now dominate the globe. He does not say much about reducing the size of corporations or human greed. This is an oversight that essentially makes him an eighteenth century philosopher in the twenty-first century. But it also makes him a secessionist, and, as such, this humanist and environmentalist has acquired some strange bedfellows among modern Confederate sympathizers.

Had it ended there, I would not have written this column. But when I opened my *Post and Courier* to the op-ed page on April 5, I was astounded to learn that Sale is not only dwelling among us in Mt. Pleasant, but he has become a serious historical revisionist. Specifically, Sale opined in a full-length column that slavery was not the cause of the Civil War, relying on that hoary old sophistry that somehow the war had nothing to do with slavery until Lincoln signed the Emancipation Proclamation on January 1, 1863.

Sale writes: "The great falsehood that the Union was fighting for a high moral cause, the elimination of chattel slavery for 4 million people ... was a myth concocted later in the war when the war was going poorly for the North."

Such a reading of history suggests a failure to grasp the passions and nuances of the times.

Everybody, North and South, black and white, knew what the great issue was in the winter of 1860-61. Even before secession, Southerners in their correspondence and newspapers often referred to Northerners — all Northerners — as "abolitionists." Once the shooting started, they called the Union armies "abolitionist armies." Anybody who witnessed the fighting in Kansas in 1855, or John Brown's raid at Harpers Ferry in 1859, knew that these were proxy battles in a larger war to come, a war between North and South, between abolitionist and slaveholder.

Even the slaves themselves knew they were the object of this great conflict. When Union troops marched onto Southern soil, they were met by throngs of slaves, fleeing their plantations, knowing they could find freedom behind Union lines. Thousands of these slaves — along with many thousands of runaways living in the North — joined the Union Army to fight for their freedom and the freedom of their families. All of this was before Lincoln made it official with the stroke of a pen.

I am actually a fan of Kirkpatrick Sale. I have read a couple of his books and several of his pieces in national magazines. But in the case of last week's column in the P&C, I think he is clearly rewriting history to serve his neo-Luddite ideology. And in the process, he seems to be attracting friends he may not want to be seen with. So I would say to him, "Welcome to the 'hood, Mr. Sale. But be careful of the company you keep."

April 13, 2011

THE STATE'S SHAME
SOUTH CAROLINA CONTINUES TO NEGLECT THE I-95 CORRIDOR

I like numerical rankings. Of course, they do not tell the whole story. Just as a ballplayer's batting and fielding stats tell you nothing about his attitude and leadership in the clubhouse, a state's or county's rankings in such quality-of-life indices as income, education, teen pregnancy, infant mortality, or violence are only part of the story. But it's a useful and important part. That's why the sports pages are filled with statistics, and census data is such a goldmine for people trying to understand what this country is about.

For years I have used this column to present an array of state rankings, most of which are less than flattering to the sovereign State of South Carolina. I have done this to demonstrate that there is something fundamentally wrong with the attitudes, the governance, and the leadership of this state. Nothing will change most of these statistics — not tax cuts, not shiny new factories from Europe and Asia, not NCAA championship sports teams, nothing — until there is a change in the way South Carolinians think about themselves and each other.

There are some new statistics out from the Robert Wood Johnson Foundation and the Population Health Institution at the University of Wisconsin. The good news is that the study does not compare us to any other states. The bad news is that South Carolina statistics can be pretty grim all by themselves.

The annual County Health Rankings and Roadmaps program breaks down each state by county to compare the rates of morbidity and mortality. There are abundant breakouts for a number of health-related factors, such as smoking and fatal car crashes. In short, the website is for healthcare professionals what Bill James' *Great American Baseball Stat Book* is for fans of the game. To look at the County Health Rankings map of South Carolina is to see a living picture of our state's history, as well as its modern demographics and most contentious issues.

The more urban areas of the state are home to the healthiest populations, reflecting their greater medical, educational, and public health resources. Moving away from the cities, the countryside becomes deadly, with up to four times the morbidity and mortality levels as in the cities and suburbs.

Particularly telling is the swath of counties running from the North Carolina border in the Pee Dee region of the state down to the Georgia border in the southern corner. Some people call it the I-95 corridor, but it has another name: the Corridor of Shame.

These are some of the poorest counties in the U.S. — majority black and culturally and economically cut off from the rest of the country and the future. They reflect the history of the region, when slaves planted and harvested vast tracts there. With the collapse of plantation agriculture, the local economy collapsed. Because it was below the fall line, it was not suitable for early industrialization. There was nothing there to attract tourism. And so the region has languished, a third world country in our midst.

The name, Corridor of Shame, refers to the public schools there. They are among the worst in the nation. The schools there are literally falling down with age, decrepitude, and the indifference of the Republican-led, white-majority government in Columbia. The 2006 documentary film *Corridor of Shame* drew nationwide attention to the problem of the schools, and Sen. Barack Obama visited the then-111-year-old J.V. Martin Middle School in Dillon County during his quest for the White House in 2008.

And now the County Health Rankings map shows us what we should already know. People are dying there faster than elsewhere in the state. Disease is endemic to the region, and it is part of the pathological cycle of poverty, ignorance, and despair. Sick people cannot work and do not want to go to school.

In East Africa right now, there is another wave of famine gripping the land. But like the previous famines, it is caused not by lack of food but by lack of distribution — usually abetted by war. In other words, famine is man-made.

The same can be said for the Corridor of Shame and all the pathologies that infest it. It will take a number of things to break the ancient cycle that grips the region, but the most important is money. In 2010, Gov. Mark Sanford rejected $700 million in federal stimulus funds bound for this state to make a political point and to boost his White House ambitions. He accomplished neither, but part of his legacy will be the Corridor of Shame, which still runs across the state like an angry scar.

You can see that scar in the County Health Rankings map.

April 11, 2012

(J.V. Martin School was replaced in 2012 with a new school, thanks to loans and a grant from the Obama Administration.)

CORRUPTION OF THE INNOCENT
MARY C. SIMMS OLIPHANT'S TROUBLING HISTORY OF SOUTH CAROLINA

Many observers have written over the years that South Carolina seems to inhabit some parallel universe, a place of different facts, different truths, maybe even a whole different reality than the rest of the United States. Here in the Palmetto State, a large number of white people still insist that the Civil War was fought over something other than slavery, that the Confederate flag has nothing to do with the state's racist heritage, and that race relations here are just hunky-dory.

There are many reasons — both cultural and institutional — for these popular delusions. My favorite malefactor is Mary C. Simms Oliphant. The name will sound familiar to many South Carolinians of a certain age. She was the granddaughter of William Gilmore Simms, the enormously popular nineteenth-century novelist, Southern nationalist, and defender of slavery. More importantly, she wrote the official state history used in South Carolina's public schools for half a century. My parents used Oliphant's books in the 1930s; I used them in the 1960s. Generations of minds were warped by their racist and Southern apologist attitudes.

These are some of the things I learned from my 1958 edition of *The History of South Carolina*: "The Africans were used to a hot climate," Oliphant wrote. "They made fine workers under the Carolina sun." Oliphant defended slaveholders and their "peculiar institution" this way: "Africans were brought from a worse life to a better one. As slaves, they were trained in the ways of civilization. Above all, the landowners argued, the slaves were given the opportunity to become Christians in a Christian land, instead of remaining heathen in a savage country."

Oliphant felt that slavery was a necessary but benign institution and described it this way: "Most masters treated their slaves kindly ... the law required the master to feed his slaves, clothe them properly, and care for them when they were sick." Elsewhere, she writes, "Most slaves were treated well, if only because it was to the planter's interest to have them healthy and contented." That there were so few slave uprisings in South Carolina "speaks well for both whites and Negroes," she writes.

During and immediately after the Civil War, Oliphant writes, "The Negroes for the most part stayed on the plantations or farms … The relationship between the whites and Negroes on the plantations was at this time very friendly. Most of the slaves had proved their affection and loyalty to their masters … For more than four years the women and children had remained on the land with only the Negroes to protect them."

But things soon changed. Here is Oliphant's very unreconstructed view of Reconstruction: "For the following eight years South Carolina was governed largely by a ruthless band of thieves." Carpetbaggers "took advantage of the ignorance and lack of experience of the Negroes … Those who did not vote Republican were threatened and mistreated. Moreover, the Republicans had the encouragement of Congress and the backing of federal troops." Oliphant adds, "The new legislature was made up chiefly of carpetbaggers, scalawags, and Negroes under their influence … Many members of the legislature could neither read nor write."

But truth and justice were restored, Oliphant assured her young charges, by men in hoods and robes: "The sight of the mounted klansmen in their white robes was enough to terrorize the Negroes. When the courts did not punish Negroes who were supposed to have committed crimes, the Klan punished them."

Later editions of Oliphant's book were somewhat toned down, but this was by and large the official history of South Carolina — taught to black students as well as white — until 1984.

Oliphant's primary way of dealing with black people in South Carolina history was to ignore them. In her 432-page text are hundreds of illustrations, yet blacks are depicted in only nine. Of those nine, two show blacks picking cotton, one is a nineteenth-century engraving showing blacks running a cotton gin, while another shows blacks hauling cotton bails on the wharves in Charleston.

The only black person identified by name in the entire book is Denmark Vesey, the accused organizer of a failed slave revolt in 1822.

The keepers of South Carolina's history, archives, and monuments have been ignoring black people for generations. This weekend we begin to correct that with two days of scholarship and observances honoring Civil War hero and Reconstruction reformer Robert Smalls. It is part of the Civil War sesquicentennial observance in the city where that terrible conflict began. The organizers of this four-year series of events are determined to avoid the mistakes of the centennial observance 50 years ago. These events will be dignified and historically inclusive. This weekend's observance will be a small step toward understanding that war and its aftermath.

May 9, 2012

UNDERSTANDING VIOLENCE
AS AMERICAN AS CHERRY PIE

It's the killing season in Charleston, as it is in much of the United States this summer. It happens every year about this time. The gunshots ring through the night. The blue lights flash. The media report another death — usually a young black man — somewhere on America's streets.

I got my introduction to Charleston violence on a sultry August night in 2002, four months after moving here. On that night, 13-year-old Velvet Brown was gunned down on Sumter Street, less than three blocks from my apartment, in a drive-by shooting.

Within days, five witnesses had identified a man named Earl Allen as the shooter, and he was charged and arrested. But when Allen came up for trial 15 months later, the witnesses had recanted their statements, and the prosecutor had no choice but to drop the charges. No one has been tried for the murder of Velvet Brown.

Earl Allen's last 15 minutes of fame came at 2 a.m. on the

morning of June 4, 2006, in a burst of gunfire near the corner of Rutledge Avenue and Strawberry Lane, six blocks from the place Velvet Brown died. The man who killed him was awaiting trial on another murder charge.

Most of the murder in Charleston is black-on-black, of course. It scars and traumatizes Charleston and almost every American city. But where does it come from? I got a look into the violent soul of South Carolina in a recent trip to Edgefield, the hometown of the late Sen. Strom Thurmond.

In 1856, one George D. Tillman killed an unarmed young man named Henry Christian over a faro game in the Planter's Hotel on the town square. Tillman was a member of the state House of Representatives at the time. He served two years for the killing in county jail, where he continued to practice law. The women of the town even brought him his meals. He later served in the state Senate and the U.S. House of Representatives.

There was also the business of Becky Cotton, "the Devil in Petticoats," who murdered three husbands and was finally dispatched by her own brother, fearing that he might be her next victim.

At least three men were killed in shoot-outs on the Edgefield town square in the nineteenth century, and when they weren't fighting and killing in front of the courthouse, the men of Edgefield carried their violence with them. Rep. Preston Brooks became a hero of the South in 1856 when he caned and nearly killed Massachusetts Sen. Charles Sumner in the U.S. Senate chamber. Lt. Gov. James H. Tillman walked out of the Statehouse in Columbia on January 15, 1903, encountered his nemesis Narciso Gonzales, editor of *The State* newspaper, and shot him to death at the corner of Gervais and Main streets.

I learned this dark history not by digging through county archives and newspapers. It is proudly recorded on murals and historical markers on the town square of Edgefield, where a life-size bronze statue of Thurmond stands.

During the first half of the nineteenth century, according to one study, rural South Carolina had a murder rate four times as high as that of urban Massachusetts. The rate in Edgefield was thought by one scholar to be perhaps twice that of South Carolina as a whole. Whereas New York City averaged three to seven murders per 100,000 people, Edgefield's antebellum murder rate was estimated at 18 per 100,000 — higher than in any place in modern America.

If violence is as American as cherry pie, as Black Panther H. Rap Brown famously said, perhaps it's actually more Southern than American. In his book, *All God's Children: The Bosket Family and the American Tradition of Violence*, Pulitzer Prize-winning journalist Fox Butterfield focuses on a young black New York City career criminal and murderer named Willie Bosket. Butterfield traces Bosket's family back five generations to Edgefield County, to an ancestor who was owned by former Gov. Andrew Pickens. He was sold several times and separated from his wife and children. He once saw a relative lynched by a white mob.

The ancestor was violent toward his own family and neighbors, and that violence, Butterfield argues, has passed down from generation to generation. The arrogance and violence of the Southern planter class — whereby a man could be killed for the smallest insult or misunderstanding — was handed down to their slaves and the children of their slaves. We hear echoes of this ancient Southern legacy in the incident two weeks ago at a local Waffle House in which two people were shot, one fatally. Witnesses say the dispute started over a cigarette.

We are all prisoners of the past, but the past is never over, not for Southerners. We have to live it every day.

July 25, 2012

FEAR & GOVERNANCE

"As early as 1820, the state seemed to possess a unique (read deviant) political culture with a prickly politics as its effective side. Historians long have asked why South Carolina's politics were so obstructionist, its politicians so petulant....[S]uch a small, socially diverse state created an internal politics so harmonious and an external politics so relentless as to be famous for both."

— *Historian Rebecca Starr*

SEEKING THE CREATIVE CLASS
GOV. SANFORD DOESN'T KNOW WHERE IT IS OR WHAT IT LOOKS LIKE

A recent issue of *South Carolina Magazine* featured the first in a series of columns by His Excellency Mark Sanford, Governor of the sovereign State of South Carolina. I don't believe for a minute that the Guv actually sat down at his computer and hacked out this forgettable piece of self-promotion, but his name and face are on it, so I hold him personally responsible.

The staffer who wrote these nuggets must have been trying mightily to impress the boss, or the editors of *SCM*. In the first paragraph, he cited author Richard Florida and his thought-provoking 2002 book, *The Rise of the Creative Class.*

He writes: "...wealth creation in the 21st Century will largely be driven by the creative process of redesigning, marketing and innovating products. This 'creative class,' Florida argues, will gravitate toward areas that boast a good quality of life. In other words, the way we look and feel as a state is increasingly a point of competitive advantage, which is why our administration has been focused on protecting and improving South Carolina's unique quality of life."

At this point the column turns surreal as the ghostwriter describes how the Sanford administration is repackaging and marketing tourism to make it fun and attractive to a whole new bunch of people.

Yes, I said tourism. Like wake-up calls and free continental breakfasts. Like crisp, clean linens and well-trimmed fairways.

If the author of this misbegotten column had bothered to read Florida's book, he would have known that tourism is one of the lowest-paying industries in the country and the very antithesis of the high-paying creative culture that the governor says he wants for our state. To make his point, Florida singles out Las Vegas, the Tourism Capital of the Universe. Las Vegas stood at 47 on Florida's creativity ranking of the 49 largest cities in America. New Orleans, another tourist hot spot, ranked 42.

So who makes up the Creative Class? According to Florida, it includes scientists and engineers, architects and designers, writers, artists, musicians, and anyone else who uses creativity as a key factor in their work in business or the professions. The Creative Class comprises 38 million members and more than 30 percent of the nation's workforce. It will continue to shape our economy and culture for generations.

How is South Carolina doing in its quest to attract this dynamic new class?

Florida writes: "One of the oldest pieces of conventional wisdom ... says the key to economic growth is attracting and retaining companies — the bigger the company the better — because companies create jobs and people go where the jobs are."

Sound familiar? That's right. Over the past 35 years, our state and local governments have thrown hundreds of millions of dollars at any company that would promise to come here and build a plant.

Has it worked? Well, that depends on what you mean by "work." I'm sure a few people would say that giving them millions of dollars for doing what they intended to do anyway is just swell. But South Carolina still has the worst public education in the nation. We still have among the lowest standards of living and personal income. We still have among the shortest life expectancies and highest infant mortality rates. Go down the list of quality-of-life indexes and South Carolina remains among the worst places to live, based on all quantifiable data.

Quality of life — including an atmosphere of tolerance and diversity — is the key to attracting the Creative Class. Indeed, Florida offers what he calls a Gay Index, showing high densities of gays correlating very closely with the nation's creativity hot spots.

"My conclusion," Florida writes, "was that rather than being driven exclusively by companies, economic growth was occurring in places that were tolerant, diverse, and open to creativity..."

Yet what do we see when we look around our state? There is a full-scale tax revolt. People are tired of paying for public education and other social services. In the last month, *The Post and Courier* has reported on a local police department that did not have the money to hire enough officers to protect its citizens and a local fire department that did not have enough equipment to protect its buildings. Do you think people don't notice things like that when they look for a place to live?

And right now our Republican legislature is counting the days until they convene in January and pass legislation to ban gay marriage.

As long as South Carolinians continue to think that cutting taxes and persecuting gays is the way to a better life, we deserve to live like a Third World country. And as long as we keep electing people like Mark Sanford and Senate Majority Leader Glenn McConnell, that's just what we will get.

October 19, 2005

THE PAST BECOMES THE FUTURE
SOUTH CAROLINA CONTINUES TO MAKE THE SAME MISTAKES

Two important stories ran on the pages of *The Post and Courier* last week and they say more than their mere text would suggest about where this state is headed and why.

The first story was that *Time* magazine ranked our own Mark Sanford among the three worst governors in the nation. The other two included the governor of Ohio, who recently pleaded guilty to criminal charges involving gifts from lobbyists; and the Louisiana governor who managed her state's response to Hurricane Katrina so badly.

Time cited the fact that Sanford's penny-pinching ways had cost the state its AAA credit rating and had brought the state's economy to a standstill. The magazine also mentioned his inability to get along with the legislature and his penchant for grandstanding, as when he carried two piglets into the Statehouse last year to protest the General Assembly's "pork-barrel spending."

"A growing chorus of critics, including leaders of his own GOP, fear that his thrift has brought the state's economy to a standstill," the two-paragraph story said. "Business leaders are losing patience with Sanford's vetoes of budget items like trade centers and tourism marketing."

Time also ranked the five best governors in the nation -- three Democrats and two Republicans.

Of course, Sanford fired back, first accusing *Time* of being a "liberal" magazine, a charge denied by College of Charleston political scientist Bill Moore. Sanford also pointed out that he had been highly praised by such conservative periodicals as *National Review* and the *Wall Street Journal* and by the right-wing Cato Institute.

Then Sanford went after the five governors who had won *Time*'s highest marks, and in so doing he demonstrated a frightening ideological fixation. Three of the top five governors had raised taxes, and Sanford's handlers didn't let it go unnoticed.

"Obviously, the way to please *Time* magazine editors is to raise taxes and the way to upset them is to fight for limited government," said one of his office flacks.

"Governor Sanford's record is clearly one of cutting taxes and limiting the size of government. Even if that upsets the liberal editors of *Time* magazine, we're confident that's the type of government the people of South Carolina are looking for."

Actually, Governor, raising taxes is not a program to piss off those pointy-headed, northern, liberal editors. It's a way of paying the bills and providing the things this state needs to maintain prosperity -- things like jobs and our AAA rating. Only a man dangerously blinded by ideology would pursue this reckless course of cutting taxes at such a high cost to the people he is supposed to serve.

But maybe it's not ideology, after all. Sanford has taken his *National Review* and Cato Institute endorsements much too seriously. He has actually started thinking of himself as presidential timber and the way to impress the leaders of the national Republican Party is to cut, cut, cut taxes at any cost.

I predict that the tax-cutting mania will play heavily into the downfall of the national Republican Party. Most Americans are sane enough to understand that at some point we have to start paying our bills and taking responsibility for the future. But if South Carolina history teaches anything, it is that South Carolinians are incapable of learning from experience. For generation after generation, we have elected demagogues, ideologues, and other fantasists; next year we will reelect Mark Sanford — not because he deserves a second term, but because he is a Republican, and white people vote Republican the way sheep are led to the abattoir.

The second bit of news — and it was a good piece of analysis by David Slade and John Frank of *The Post and Courier* — is that the so-called tax reform that the General Assembly has been working on for months is actually just another plan to enrich the rich at the expense of the rest of us.

Slade and Frank wrote: "The leading plans for property tax reform in South Carolina would give the lion's share of the benefits to those with pricey real estate, while owners of the least expensive homes could wind up paying more tax instead of less...

"Previous state efforts to reduce the real estate tax burden have been directed toward the elderly and disabled, and to homeowners with lower-priced residences, but the plans under review would cut real estate taxes without regard to property value or the owner's age or income."

There are a number of reasons why the South is so backward and economically underdeveloped. One is that we continue to elect flamboyant populists, who are ineffective at the art of governance. The other is that we refuse to tax the people who can afford it — i.e., the rich — for the money it costs to be a modern, developed society.

We saw two good examples of these phenomena last week.

November 23, 2005

SAFE UNTIL JANUARY
THE LEGISLATIVE SESSION ENDS, BUT NOT SOON ENOUGH

The late Sol Blatt — who was speaker of the state House of Representatives almost as long as Strom Thurmond was in the U.S. Senate — liked to quote his father as saying, "No man is safe in his person or his property as long as the legislature is in session."

Well, we can relax. The General Assembly has done all the damage it can and gone home to make new mischief. A number of bills and acts came out of the legislative session that I could probably write whole columns about, but I will focus on three and hope to make my point. And, as always, that point is that this poor old state is stuck with two wheels in the ditch because we keep electing the same sorry people, who keep making the same bad policy, generation after generation.

Let's start with our brand-new law authorizing the death penalty for serial child rapists. Yes, our solons stood up to the powerful child rapist lobby and said, "Enough is enough!" Not that we have had a rash of serial rapists of children under the age of 11 — or that we have had even one, that I am aware of. But when we find one, by God, we'll be ready!

Never mind that the law is probably unconstitutional. (South Carolinians famously have little regard for the Constitution.) The U.S. Supreme Court has ruled that the death penalty, employed to punish non-homicidal crimes, constitutes cruel and unusual punishment.

Our state's top lawyer, Attorney General Henry McMaster, might have cautioned the zealous lawmakers that they were treading on thin ice. But McMaster was out front, leading the bandwagon, intoning piously and pompously, "This is a great step forward that will send a message loud and clear that that kind of conduct is not tolerated in South Carolina. We have stepped into the forefront of those states recognizing the threat of sexual predators."

It's a good thing we are in the forefront of something, for South Carolina is certainly not in the forefront of providing a safe and livable environment for our children. What masks itself as a child-protection law has nothing to do with protecting children. If the General Assembly gave a damn about our kids, South Carolina wouldn't rank 42nd in the nation in overall well-being of its children, as determined by the annual Kids Count Survey. We wouldn't have the fourth-highest rate of low birth-weight babies in the nation and 23 percent of our children wouldn't live in poverty. If our legislators cared about children, we wouldn't have the worst SAT scores in the nation and we wouldn't rank 47th in the percentage of high school graduates or have the 11th highest percentage of teen smokers.

No, this law has nothing to do with protecting children. This is an anti-sex law, just like the bill introduced by Rep. Ralph Davenport (R-Spartanburg) to outlaw sex toys in this Bible-thumping province; just like the proposed constitutional amendment to ban gay marriage; just like dozens of other laws over the years whose purpose it was to codify who may have sex with whom, in what position, and under what circumstances. Be assured, if God doesn't punish your sins, the State of South Carolina will.

The General Assembly gave us another solution in search of a problem, this one in the form of a law making it a crime to protest within 1,000 feet of a funeral. Nothing like that has happened in South Carolina and there is little reason to suspect that it will, but like a troop of Boy Scouts on a backyard camp-out, our legislators are prepared.

Finally, there is the "property tax relief act." Designed primarily to lower property taxes for wealthy coastal homeowners, the law replaces lost revenues by raising the sales tax on everybody else by two percent, giving South Carolina one of the most regressive tax structures in the nation. (As a bone to the poor, the lawmakers thoughtfully lowered the sales tax on groceries from five percent to three percent, forgetting that poor people also wear clothes, drive cars and consume a host of other goods that will now cost more.)

Will the higher sales tax offset the reduced property tax? Maybe, maybe not. But it doesn't seem too important, because the law was carefully drawn to stipulate that the property tax "relief" comes out of that portion of the tax that goes to fund school operations. So if the new tax structure doesn't work, well, what the heck. It's only education anyway.

So there you have it: It's been a busy year for our General Assembly. And they will be back to serve us again in January.

June 21, 2006

(Ralph Davenport's "dildo bill" did not get out of committee, but the amendment to ban gay marriage was adopted in referendum by a 2-to-1 margin.)

LIVING IN THE THIRD WORLD, PART 1
WELCOME TO SOUTH CAROLINA, WHERE POVERTY IS POLICY

In the next weeks, we are going to be hearing a lot from Gov. Mark Sanford about the huge amount of new investment his administration has brought to the state over the last four years. In 2002, we heard the same boasts from Gov. Jim Hodges.

In fact, South Carolina has attracted billions of dollars worth of factories, shipping and receiving centers, and other investments in recent decades. And that's good, because — if we know anything from listening to the echo chamber in Columbia — new investment means jobs and jobs mean prosperity and prosperity means a better standard of living for South Carolinians. And with enough new investment and jobs and prosperity, maybe this little state can crawl out of the cellar of national rankings and have something to crow about.

And yet, year after year, despite all this "progress," the dismal record shows that South Carolina remains near the bottom in personal income, standard of living, educational attainment, SAT scores, life expectancy, environmental quality ... and the list goes on. Year after year, our unemployment rate remains one of the highest in the nation. Our leaders turn our state into one vast industrial park and proclaim, "Jobs, jobs, jobs for all," but South

Carolina remains a Third World country and a national laughing-stock. Have you ever wondered why?

We got a little insight into this paradox in the September 3 issue of *The State*. On a single page were reports that Mike Campbell, son of the late Gov. Carroll Campbell, who lost a recent bid for the GOP nomination for lieutenant governor, will head up the new state chapter of Americans for Prosperity, a Washington-based, pro-business, free-market lobbying group; and the S.C. Chamber of Commerce is joining with three other pro-business, right wing organizations to create the Coalition Against Unlimited Spending, a group to lobby for lower taxes.

From its high-rise offices looking down on the Statehouse, the S.C. Chamber of Commerce and its 4,500 members bring enormous muscle to bear on the General Assembly. Thanks to that muscle, South Carolina has among the lowest corporate taxes, lowest environmental standards, and absolutely the lowest rate of unionized labor in the nation. Two years ago, the General Assembly treated its corporate underwriters with an even stronger "employment at will" law, clarifying that employers have the final say in who works and under what circumstances, leaving employees few rights in their relationship with their employers.

According to its 2005 Annual Report, the S.C. Chamber of Commerce successfully lobbied the General Assembly for $835 million in tax cuts for businesses in the legislative session. Indeed, as a record number of businesses were lured into the state during the 1990s, total corporate income tax revenue fell by six percent! Local property tax revenue on business equipment fell by 13 percent between 1993 and 1997, according to Suzan Erem, who has researched state business and labor practices for a forthcoming book.

"South Carolina has always been a very conservative state, very pro-business," Chamber of Commerce president Howard Hunter told Erem. "When I was at the Department of Revenue, before I came here, South Carolina was the only state that carried its tax administrator on its trade missions because we had such a positive tax climate for business."

South Carolina is a "right-to-work" state, which helps keep unions weak. The S.C. Chamber of Commerce website boasts the state's low percentage of organized labor. What it doesn't mention is that our state ranks 45th in both per capita income and in hourly earnings in manufacturing, and has the eighth highest level of poverty in the nation. It doesn't mention that workers in non-right-to-work states make 18 percent more than their counterparts in right-to-work states.

Keeping people poor is what draws industry to South Carolina and the people who run this state do not want to upset that sweet little apple cart. They also don't want to raise taxes on industry, which means that someone else has to pay those taxes, and, of course, that someone else is the group of people who already rank 45th in per capita income and hourly earnings in the nation.

Furthermore, South Carolina's antiquated income tax structure is one of the most regressive in the nation, impoverishing the poor and enriching the rich. The income tax inequity was compounded recently with passage of "property tax reform," which protects wealthy property owners by raising the sales tax on everyone, including the poor.

South Carolina's economy is designed to be unfair and inequitable — and as *The State* reported recently, powerful interests are working hard to make it more so. Until environmental and labor groups can compete with the wealth and resources of the business lobby, we will continue to live in a Third World state.

September 13, 2006

LIVING IN THE THIRD WORLD, PART 2
ATTITUDE IS EVERYTHING

You may have read the stories a few weeks ago in the *Post and Courier*: An untold number of drivers have requested "P-tags" for their personal vehicles, allowing them to park in delivery zones, greatly expanding their options in the parking-poor downtown region of the Peninsula.

These white tags, whose serial numbers start with the letter P and which are marked "Truck," have proliferated wildly in recent years, for the simple reason that citizens may obtain them by lying to the Department of Motor Vehicles and saying they have a business need for a P-tag. The state does not verify these claims and municipalities have no way of enforcing the "honor code" in the use of these tags.

A trip down King Street, between Calhoun and Broad, on any given day during business hours will probably reveal a dozen P-tags on vehicles that clearly don't need them. These vehicles have no corporate signage. There are baby seats and Saks Fifth Avenue shopping bags in some of them. What is also interesting is that the vast majority of these faux delivery trucks are expensive, late-model vehicles — BMWs, SUVs, Lexuses and the like. I have yet to see a P-tag on a clunker. This appears to be a game for the rich, perhaps because the P-tags cost a little more than regular tags, or perhaps because only a certain group of people know how to game the system.

Another story that recently caught my eye came out of New York City, where U.N. diplomats from around the world have famously abused their parking privileges for years. They park wherever they please for as long as they please and when they come back to their cars, they make confetti of their parking tickets. It's called diplomatic immunity. It's an ancient tradition among nations and it has found a special place of grievance in Gotham.

Now a new study by a couple of economists from Columbia University and the University of California-Berkeley sheds new light on this tradition. It seems that diplomats from governments with a high level of corruption are the worst abusers of diplomatic parking immunity, according to the study's authors.

The study focused on diplomatic parking violations from November 1997 through October 2002 and what it revealed was, well, revealing. Diplomats from low-corruption countries, such as Norway, behaved "remarkably well even in situations where they can get away with violations," the study found. Those from high-corruption counties, such as Nigeria, committed many violations, "suggesting that they bring the social norms or corruption culture of their home country with them to New York City."

The 10 worst parking violators were Kuwait, Egypt, Chad, Sudan, Bulgaria, Mozambique, Albania, Angola, Senegal, and Pakistan. These and other countries accumulated some 150,000 parking tickets, representing some $18 million in unpaid fines. Others had high rates, but paid their fines. These included Turkey, Bahrain, Malaysia, and Oman.

On the other end of the spectrum, Sweden, Norway, Denmark, Japan, Canada, and Israel had no parking violations.

Need I point out that the countries with the most parking violations are among the most socially and economically backward places on the planet, while the countries with the fewest violations are highly developed economically, and they are relative models of democracy and transparency?

In the abstract of their study, the scholars wrote: "Corruption is believed to be a major factor impeding economic development ... the importance of legal enforcement versus cultural norms in controlling corruption is poorly understood."

Of course, corruption is in the eye of the beholder. What is corrupt in one culture is simply business as usual in another. I prefer to use a broad definition of corruption and it goes something like this: "Any use of social or political position by one group or individual to advance itself over another group or individual." By this definition, South Carolina is probably the most corrupt province west of Bombay. Our corruption would include slavery, segregation, the historic disenfranchisement of blacks and poor whites, a constitutional structure with power centered in Columbia, school vouchers, a regressive tax code, and hundreds of other laws and customs most South Carolinians don't even think about. Corruption is so endemic in this state that it is considered, well, business as usual. And the people who lie to state authorities to get their P-tags probably don't think of themselves as corrupt. They are just playing the game the way they have always been taught to play it.

But the price we pay for this casual corruption is a permanently broken economy and a racially and economically divided society. Remember that the next time you see a P-tag on a $60,000 BMW.

September 20, 2006

ANOTHER LESSON FROM HISTORY
IN SOUTH CAROLINA, TAX CUTS ARE FOR THE RICH

Historian Walter Edgar has pointed out that South Carolina was founded by a group of planters from Barbados who brought their oligarchic attitudes with them. Those attitudes are still alive and well among us.

The Barbadians created a top-down society, with the plantation as the basic unit of political power. Later the cotton mill replaced the plantation. Today the corporation is the center of power in this very conservative state. But whatever the age or the nature of the economy, the state's political power has always been from the top down, and democracy has never been more than window dressing.

That was never more obvious than with the General Assembly's recent tax-writing policy. First, let's take a look at the $81 million income-tax cut the white Republican majority in the House just voted to give to the wealthiest South Carolinians.

The tax cut is part of the $7.3 billion state budget. Democrats tried to block the income tax cut, saying that the money could be spent on so many things, including education, better roads, Medicaid, or new school buses for our children. This was a particularly pointed argument in light of *The Post and Courier*'s recent series of stories, detailing how the state's school bus fleet is the oldest, most dangerous, most polluting in the nation.

The House did vote to direct some money to that problem and to rotate out the state's decrepit school bus fleet *over the next 15 years*! But nothing could dissuade the GOPers who run the legislature from cutting the income tax.

"Republicans are about cutting taxes -- that's what we do," Rep. Dan Cooper (R-Piedmont) said. But Rep. Vida Miller (D-Georgetown) said that she had never had a constituent ask her for income tax relief in her 10 years in Columbia. And why should she? South Carolina has one of the lowest income taxes in the nation.

An analysis by the State Revenue Department shows that the tax cut would mean a $35 savings for a family of four with an adjusted gross income of $45,000 a year; $130 savings for a family earning $100,000; and $1,638 for a family with income of $1 million.

Democrats argued, instead of income tax relief for the wealthy, why not cut property taxes or cut the sales tax on groceries, where it would be felt by those who need it most? But Republicans would have none of that.

With no groundswell of support for an income tax cut, with so many critical needs going unfunded in this backward, undeveloped state, why would Republican lawmakers insist on this tax cut so clearly engineered to benefit the rich?

There is only one explanation: They were listening to their DNA. They were following an ancient South Carolina imperative which dictates that government exists to serve power and wealth.

This same sad tradition is the basis of the funding crisis the Charleston County School District now faces.

Under the budget now being considered in the House, CCSD stands to lose more than $15 million in funding under the formula of the Education Finance Act. These cuts are being proposed because the Republican-led General Assembly is still trying to work out the details of the change in public education funding from a system based primarily on property taxes to a system based on the new sales tax law that was passed last year.

Under this complex EFA formula, Charleston County is one of five districts slated to receive a deficit in funding this year. The funding crisis is compounded by the fact that the state has added requirements for an additional $12 million in spending. Between reduced funding and additional spending mandates, Charleston County School District is looking at a deficit between $25 million and $32 million for fiscal year 2008.

What is this EFA formula?

Last year, the General Assembly passed the Property Tax Revaluation Reform Act, dramatically changing funding for public education in South Carolina. Among other things, it increased the sales tax to offset a reduction in property tax, the traditional source of most education funding.

The General Assembly has determined that Charleston County has the highest property values in the state to support its schools, and therefore the least need for supplemental state funding from the state Homestead Exemption Fund. Fair enough. But last year's property tax relief – aimed at relieving taxes for the wealthiest property owners in the state -- also capped the millage rate on the most expensive property in the county. Charleston County Schools are caught in a double-whammy: The high property tax base makes it ineligible for state supplemental funding, yet that same tax base is undermined by the millage cap on property tax.

School children lose and the wealthy win again. And history repeats itself, as it always does in South Carolina.

March 28, 2007

AN ACT OF LEGISLATIVE FRAUD
LEGISLATORS UNDERCUT HOME RULE, WORKER SAFETY

The South Carolina General Assembly has always been an arrogant lot. Before the 1960s, they did not even pretend to be democratically elected. Today they do pretend, but it's a shabby charade.

To wit: The House and Senate bills that would run roughshod over Home Rule and overturn nine local smoke-free ordinances which were passed in the last year by Greenville, Columbia, Charleston, Beaufort County, and other municipalities.

The ordinances were designed to protect workers by making workplaces smoke-free. They were spurred in part by a June 2006 U.S. Surgeon General's report that found even the most sophisticated ventilation systems cannot eliminate secondhand smoke from the air. There is no safe level of secondhand smoke, the Surgeon General said.

Municipalities may have also been motivated by a couple of recent polls. A statewide survey, conducted by Public Opinion Strategies and released in February 2006, found that 68 percent of registered voters favor smoke-free workplaces. The same poll showed that 59 percent of voters favor letting local communities decide whether to pass laws to control smoking in workplaces.

Another poll, conducted by a public policy and research branch of the University of South Carolina, in December 2005, found that 70 percent of Charleston residents would support a city law prohibiting smoking inside all workplaces, including bars and restaurants. Additionally, 72 percent of Charleston residents favored giving local communities the option of passing their own laws to restrict smoking in public places, even if those laws may be stronger than the state law.

In passing the two bills — S.186 and H.3119 — out of committee, the General Assembly seems intent on telling the citizens of South Carolina to go to hell. They intend to overturn local smoke-free ordinances and ignore public opinion to establish a statewide "Clean Indoor Air Act."

Any business that tried to sell a product as egregiously misnamed and duplicitously advertised as the Clean Indoor Air Act would be subject to criminal or civil liability.

The Clean Indoor Air Act is anything but. This piece of legislation has been bought and paid for by the tobacco industry, whose lobbyists have filled the Statehouse like carpetbaggers for weeks. The push is on to get the bills out of their respective committees by the May 1 deadline so that they may be voted on by the full chambers before the end of the legislative session. Otherwise, the tobacco industry will have to wait until next year to ram this dirty law through the legislature.

"I would hope (the legislators) would be prudent and hear what the public has to say before passing this law," said Dan Carrigan, executive director of the Smoke Free Action Network, "but the tobacco industry wants their payoff now."

And what will this Clean Indoor Air Act accomplish? It will supersede local laws — such as Charleston's — that ban smoking in all places of business with one or more employees. That includes bars and restaurants.

The Clean Indoor Air Act would allow bars and restaurants to convert to smoking establishments during business hours that they choose and post those hours on the door. For this legal sleight-of-hand they would have to obtain a $100 state permit. During smoking hours, children would be prohibited from entering the restaurant.

"They would put the children out in order to protect the smokers," Carrigan said.

According to Carrigan, the tobacco industry has been working around the nation to get state legislatures to pass preemptive laws such as this one, which would take authority to regulate smoking away from local governments and put it in the legislature. The strategy makes sense for the tobacco industry, Carrigan said, because it is easier to control one state legislature than hundreds of municipalities and counties.

The tobacco industry — with the support of the S.C. Hospitality Association — is having its way with our lawmakers. Our

General Assembly is about to override local laws and push through the weakest, most fraudulent "clean air" law in the nation.

In passing the bill out of committee, some senators referred to the "voluntary risk" patrons take when entering a bar or restaurant where smoking is allowed. They did not address the involuntary risk employees face every time they go to work.

The most contemptible response came from Sen. Glenn McConnell (R-Charleston), chairman of the Judiciary Committee, who said, "Nobody stops me on the streets of Charleston and says that they want home rule."

Of course, nobody stopped him on the street to say they wanted an income tax cut for millionaires or a nearly $100 million museum to house his damned Confederate submarine. We sure as hell got that without asking.

If this fraudulent law passes, Carrigan said he will take his battle to Columbia: "This is just the beginning."

May 2, 2007

(The Clean Indoor Air Act did not get out of Senate committee. Today, more than half of all South Carolinians live in smoke-free counties and municipalities.)

HATE CRIME LEGISLATION
LET'S PUT IT ON THE AGENDA FOR NEXT YEAR

In a few days, the 2007 legislative session will be history. And it will be soon forgotten, as most legislative sessions are.

What our General Assembly is famous for doing is nothing — nothing at all. When it does rouse itself to act, it is usually in some Neanderthal rage against civil rights or women's rights, or any sign of rational awakening or global awareness. Nothing demonstrates this mentality more clearly than the Confederate flag that still flies on the lawn in front of our Statehouse.

South Carolina has paid a high price for that forlorn piece of vainglory. Due to the boycott by the National Association for the Advancement of Colored People (NAACP), we have lost hundreds of millions of dollars in tourism, conventions, trade shows, and sporting events.

Yet, the flag is still there. On newspaper op-ed pages around the state recently, Charleston's own Sen. Glenn McConnell said the flag will remain in front of the Statehouse, so there is no use complaining about it. "No one can persuasively argue that it represents bigotry or slavery," he wrote. "Symbols are defined by the people who display them — and by the context of their use."

The American Nazi Party was persuaded that the flag has everything to do with bigotry and slavery. That's why they chose the Statehouse steps in Columbia for a national rally last month. The Nazi presidential candidate praised the flag, while his fans cheered and displayed their own Confederate flags around him.

At the same time the Nazis chose Columbia for their rally, that strange group called Christian Exodus was stepping up its efforts to bring radical Christian separatists to South Carolina from around the country, with the idea of eventually taking over local governments, then the state government, and imposing a Bible-based "Christian" legal code. In a Christian Exodus state, there would be no room for dissent, diversity, or minority views. As Christian Exodus leader Corey Burnell has said, "The majority will vote and the majority will rule. Those in disagreement can relocate or change their ideas to fit with the majority." And if the federal government has any problem with this, Burnell and his followers are willing and ready to secede. Isn't that what the Confederate flag is all about?

There is no question that South Carolina has an image problem. We are sending out a lot of very bad vibes, and a lot of very ugly people are responding by coming here. Tsk, tsk. What's a poor state to do?

Well, I think it's time we change our image and if we can't bring down the Flag of Shame, then it's time to pass a hate crime law. It's much too late to get it on the agenda for this legislative session, but it should be first in line for consideration when the solons return to Columbia in January.

After all, South Carolina is one of only three states that does not have a hate crime statute, while 15 other states protect other minorities, but not gays. The murder of a young gay man on the street in front of a Greenville bar on May 17 indicates the need for such a law. State murder charges have been brought against an 18-year-old man for striking and killing 20-year-old Sean William Kennedy "without legal provocation with implication that this was the result of the defendant not liking the sexual identity of the victim," according to the convoluted language of the murder warrant. The killing is also being investigated by the FBI, which may bring hate crime charges, since the state has no such authority.

Of course, any attempt to pass hate crime legislation in this state will meet fierce resistance from the Christian Right. Right-wing Christians have adopted hate-crime legislation as one of their rallying points. Today they are mobilized against a new federal hate crime law, which the White House has said it will veto if it gets out of Congress.

Rabid Christians have attacked the bill as anti-Christian and pro-terrorist. They claim that ministers will be jailed for criticizing gays and parents will be jailed for disciplining their children. Not surprisingly, this malicious nonsense has made its way onto the pages of the *Post and Courier* in a May 13 letter to the editor.

Passing this federal hate crime legislation would be an act of faith in our own best nature. And passing a state hate crime law would send a powerful signal that South Carolinians will not be bullied by the worst elements among us. We owe it to ourselves and to the rest of the country.

May 30, 2007

(South Carolina still has no hate crime law in 2015.)

A PEEK INSIDE
THE WHITE SOUTHERN MIND
DORCHESTER COUNTY COUNCIL REJECTS HEALTHCARE RESOLUTION

"Dorchester County Council rescinded a resolution for more affordable health insurance Tuesday after complaints that it sounded too much like what Democrats have been proposing."

—*The Post and Courier,* September 5, 2007

Dorchester County has the reputation of being one of the most Republican places in one of the most Republican states in the nation.

How else to explain the logic of what council did last week? First, they endorsed an idea on its merits. Then they rescinded it because it sounded like something the Democrats might do!

"It was an honorable intent," Councilmember Mike Murphree said of the resolution. "But when I read it more, it started to sound more and more like Hillary (Clinton) care. I think this is an issue that needs to be left to the Democrats, and I don't want to be associated with them."

So there you have it! It seems Mr. Murphree would rather look stupid than be associated with Democrats. After all, the resolution affirming a "health care crisis caused by increasing numbers of uninsured people, skyrocketing costs and limited access" seemed like a good idea two weeks earlier, when Murphree and a majority of county council endorsed it. And who could argue with calling on elected officials and candidates to "work together with consumers, businesses, and health care providers to ensure quality, affordable health care for everyone"?

Apparently Murphree and three other county council Republicans suddenly found it objectionable. I would bet my shoes that none of them saw Michael Moore's documentary *Sicko*. One of the points that Moore makes is that the American Medical Association and other corporate interests have long used scare tactics and buzz words like "socialized medicine" to frighten Americans away from better health care.

Murphree explained to *The Post and Courier* that he discovered the resolution is being driven by national and state organizations acting under the umbrella of the Service Employees International Union, which is pushing health care reform. Apparently that was enough to flip the four Republicans and kill the resolution.

What we witnessed in Dorchester County last week was remarkable only in its transparency. It is a perfect example of the way white Southerners have been thinking and acting politically for many generations. Because a good idea was associated with the Service Employees International Union, it was suddenly bad. And to make sure his constituents got the idea, he tied it to another symbol of all things reprehensible to southern whites — Hillary Clinton. Such reflexive reaction to certain groups, ideas and institutions is the sign of a fearful people.

Living in fear is what southern white people have been doing for centuries and it has distorted their culture, their politics, their logic. In the mind of so many white Southerners, everything has been reduced to bumper sticker reasoning, to the absolutes of good and bad: Conservatives are good. Liberals are bad. Republicans are good. Democrats are bad. The Confederate flag is good. The NAACP is bad. White southerners can march in lock step to that cadence and never miss a beat. And when an issue is complex — as the matter of health care surely is — they need only look for an identifying tag to know whether it's good or bad. In the case of the Dorchester County resolution, it was vaguely attached to a labor union and – as almost all white Southerners can tell you – labor unions are bad, bad, bad! *Ipso facto*, the health care resolution was bad.

If you are a white politician, you must make clear to white voters how firmly, how resolutely, how irrevocably you stand on the side of good. If there is anything white southerners can't abide, it's a politician who empathizes with both sides of an issue.

In the case of Paul Campbell, who recently ran in a special election for state senate from Dorchester County, it was not enough that he tell the voters that he was a Republican. All candidates in the race, with one exception, were Republican. So Campbell had to demonstrate that he was more Republican than his rivals. He was, in fact, a "Rock Solid Republican," according to his campaign signs. He was not a "smart Republican," nor an "experienced Republican" nor a "qualified Republican." He was the most uncompromising Republican. And what was he uncompromising about? Well, that's one of those codes that nobody can explain, but white Southerners understand instinctively. They understood well enough to nominate and elect him overwhelmingly to the Senate. And I think Campbell would have understood instinctively that any health care resolution that is sponsored by a labor union is bad — no matter how reasonable it sounds.

This is the kind of logic that has been driving southern politics for centuries and until white southerners overcome their fear of the world, it will continue to hold us back.

September 12, 2007

TRAVESTY AT THE YACHT CLUB
THESE HUCKSTERS GIVE HUMANITARIANISM A BAD NAME

There they stood in their white ties and tails, cocktails in hand, looking very smug and pleased with themselves. And why shouldn't they? Not only had they just screwed the people of South Carolina out of millions of tax dollars, but they were celebrating it as a great humanitarian triumph.

The photograph in the October 27 *Post & Courier* would be funny if it were not obscene. A group of Charleston's most distinguished gentlemen were gathered at the Carolina Yacht Club for the French Society's 191st anniversary dinner. As part of their celebration they had just made their annual Humanitati Award to one Emerson Read Sr. for his efforts to "improve the human condition either in his community or the world at large," according to the *P&C*.

"Like a savior, he was there when we needed him," French Society member Jack Simmons told those gathered at the yacht club. "And by 'we' I mean every single South Carolinian and potentially every United States citizen."

So what had this great man done to earn such commendation and the manifest love and admiration of his peers? Did he find a cure for cancer? Bring peace to the Middle East? Discover a way to reverse global climate change?

No, Emerson Read led the campaign to abolish property taxes in South Carolina. He did not completely succeed. The General Assembly eliminated the school operations portion of the property tax and capped reassessment at 15 percent for residential properties that had not changed hands. In exchange, they raised the state sales tax by one percent and threw the middle class a bone by eliminating sales tax on most groceries, saving the average household about $218 a year.

While Read says his war on property tax is not finished, he has already won a substantial reduction in tax for some home owners, especially for owners of expensive houses — the kind of plutocrats and good old boys who stood around the yacht club two weeks ago, overdressed, overfed, toasting their "savior" and talking about improving the human condition.

Humanitati, my ass. In a state which already has one of the most regressive tax structures in the nation, the property tax reduction and corresponding sales tax increase was just the most recent way our lawmakers have found to steal from the middle class and give to the rich in this Third World state.

Last year, the Center for a Better South published Doing Better: *Progressive Tax Reform for the American South*, which offered 11 practical ideas for fairer taxes in the 11 states of the old Confederacy. One recommendation was to create a property tax circuit breaker to shield residents from excessive taxation by connecting property tax to an individual's ability to pay. It's a way to keep the poor and elderly from being taxed out of their homes. No southern state has a property tax circuit breaker, which is a progressive solution to excessive property tax. Yet it has worked in other states, and it could work here.

But when the legislature was debating property tax reform in 2006, it specifically threw out the circuit breaker. The reason is clear enough. The government-hating, tax-cutting Republicans do not want to make property taxes practical and workable. They want them to be onerous and oppressive, thus giving themselves an excuse to do away with them altogether. And giving a bunch of greedy blowhards down at the Carolina Yacht Club an opportunity to laud a demagogue like Emerson Read.

Why do South Carolina voters continue to fall for the sleight-of-hand tax tricks and other ruses our legislators hand us — year after year, generation after generation? In the October 16 issue of *Harper's*, writer Ken Silverstein offered an insight.

Silverstein interviewed state Republican political operative Rod Shealy ("Something Sleazy on the Isle,") and proposed a theory that the flood of new residents into South Carolina was changing the character of the electorate. As a result, running hard right in the state, on issues such as abortion and gay marriage, would become less effective. "The smart strategy is to pay lip service to social issues, but to focus on pocket book issues that appeal to fiscal conservatives," he suggested.

Shealy was doubtful. "It's true, our entire coast is filled with people who sound more like you than they do like me," he told Silverman. "But it will be a long time before it's a bad strategy to run to the right in South Carolina ... Working the social issues is still important."

South Carolina's legislators will always be working the social issues, like last November's constitutional amendment against gay marriage. And the voters in this Baptist-ridden state will always fall for it. And that's why you won't be seeing any fair tax relief here in the near future.

November 7, 2007

LIVING IN THE THIRD WORLD, PART 3
DOES THIS MAKE MARK SANFORD A BANANA REPUBLICAN?

I have been criticized over the years for referring to our fair state as a banana republic. I make no apologies, and news in the past week only confirms this harsh judgment. South Carolina is run by corporate interests, for corporate interests. What happens in the Statehouse is largely window dressing on this little Third World country we call home.

Last week, *The State* newspaper in Columbia ran a series of stories on the laxness and cronyism in the state Department of Health and Environmental Control. This is the executive agency charged with keeping our land, air, and water clean and safe. That this agency has failed in its mission is a gross understatement.

According to *The State*, DHEC has been in bed with corporate malefactors for years, relaxing regulations, looking the other way as rules were stretched and broken.

Among *The State*'s findings:

• A former DHEC investigator said he was punished by superiors for investigating an illegal asbestos dump in Swansea. He has sued DHEC, claiming that state legislators used their influence to get DHEC to back off the case. The suit names three ranking DHEC officials as defendants.

• DHEC knew in 1985 that a private utility was polluting a Richland County neighborhood's drinking water with lead, yet it did not notify the residents and did not get the lead removed until 2005. Residents have tested positive for lead in their blood.

• DHEC failed to post signs along Lowcountry rivers, warning people that fish from those waters had high levels of mercury, which may have come from coal-burning plants in the area. A number of people have tested positive for mercury in their blood, and some have become ill. DHEC has known about high mercury levels since the 1990s.

• DHEC withheld documents relating to a leaking nuclear waste landfill, saying that to release the documents to plaintiffs would violate the trade secrets of Chem-Nuclear, the company that operates the landfill. This was one example of how DHEC has reportedly failed to comply with requests for information by attorneys, citizens, media, and legislators.

• Under DHEC's stewardship, South Carolina has become the garbage mecca of the East Coast. The three largest private waste haulers in the nation operate mega-dumps here. DHEC has largely ignored residents' and legislators' complaints about the flood of garbage. "We are the pay toilet of the nation," a state senator told *The State*.

• Some of DHEC's most skilled and highly paid staffers leave the agency to go to work for the very companies they have been trained to regulate. Some refer to the agency as the "University of DHEC."

• DHEC, responsible for enforcing the state's Beachfront Management Act, has relaxed much of its regulation, giving developers the green light to build ever larger structures ever closer to the surf in popular resorts. In the absence of DHEC regulation, the Hilton Head Island town council is considering creating regulations to protect its beachfront from development.

Make no mistake — behavior such as this would prompt legislative and even criminal investigations in many states and sovereign countries. But in South Carolina, it is simply business as usual. I wager that no one will lose his job or be inconvenienced in any way by *The State*'s revelations.

And bear in mind that this travesty of environmental protection is happening on Gov. Mark Sanford's watch. In fact, it's happening under his nose. DHEC is an executive agency; its director serves at his pleasure. This regulatory sham appears to be a perfect example of Sanford's libertarian philosophy at work. Now there is increasing talk of Sanford running for president in 2012. Well, why not? If you liked George W. Bush, you'll love Mark Sanford.

Before *The State*'s series on DHEC had run its course last week, we were treated to more news of government malfeasance and public endangerment. A coalition of health organizations released a report on Tuesday saying that South Carolina ranked dead last among the states in the amount of money it spends to prevent and reduce tobacco consumption. South Carolina is budgeted to spend $1 million on prevention programs in fiscal 2009; the Centers for Disease Control recommended that we spend $62.2 million. The tobacco industry will spend more than $280 million marketing its products in our state in the fiscal year.

With such official attitudes toward public health and environmental protection, it is not surprising that this is one of the most dangerous places in the nation to live. South Carolina has the third shortest life expectancy in the country. But not to worry! The U.S. Chamber of Commerce ranks us year after year as one of the best places in America to do business.

November 26, 2008

FRIEND OF THE RICH
MARK SANFORD WANTS TO CUT THEIR INCOME TAXES

A few weeks ago I was on a panel with a couple of other local know-it-alls, discussing the significance of the recent election and what we might look for in the next four to eight years. As frequently happens in the waning minutes of panel discussions, questions and answers started drifting far afield of the original topic.

A woman raised her hand to ask, "How long will it take South Carolina to catch up with the rest of the country in economic and social development?"

I told her I had been waiting 58 years and wasn't holding my breath. The line was good for a laugh, but of course it spoke only a small fraction of the truth. I'm sure that in 1908 people were asking when South Carolina would finally arrive in the twentieth century and they went to their graves wondering.

We have been electing bad leaders in this state for generations. It's as much a part of our history and culture as iced tea and going to church on Sunday. Why does South Carolina lag behind the rest of the nation? The answer is simple: because we keep electing people like Mark Sanford.

Sanford's latest nod to nineteenth-century thinking was his proposal last week to overhaul the state's income tax structure, creating a flat tax. A flat tax is the holy grail of Republican politicians and policy-makers. It is the strychnine-laced Kool-Aid, which conservatives have been trying to get America to drink since the Reagan years. The Kool-Aid, in this case, is a simplified tax code, with all deductions and loopholes eliminated. The strychnine, well, that's a tax structure that simply won't fund a modern government with its myriad services and responsibilities.

That's why progressive governments have progressive tax structures, setting higher rates for higher income levels. The most progressive governments in the world — Scandinavia and a handful of Western European nations — have the most progressive tax structures. They also have the lowest rates of poverty and highest standards of living, along with such concomitant benefits as low levels of violence, illiteracy, and teen pregnancy.

Governments with highly regressive tax structures — like the banana republics of Latin America and the southern United States — tend to have high levels of poverty, illiteracy, and violence, as well as repressive political and social institutions. Sound familiar?

Why is South Carolina so economically and socially undeveloped? You know at least part of the reason: a tax structure that is designed to keep wealth in the hands of the wealthy at the expense of public institutions and infrastructure which benefit society as a whole. Now Mark Sanford wants to tip the economic table even more in favor of the rich.

The Post and Courier wasted no time in calling Sanford on his flat tax flimflam. Four days after the governor announced his plan, the *P&C* ran a story saying, "More than half of the families in South Carolina would not save a dime under the flat tax plan proposed by Gov. Mark Sanford, but income tax savings for the wealthy would be substantial..."

Tax savings would not kick in until the $65,000 level for a family of four. That family would save exactly $1, according to the

P&C analysis. If you are lucky enough to make $250,000 a year, you could save $6,178 under the Sanford tax plan. Where do you fit on that scale?

Incredibly, Sanford justifies this tax break for the wealthy by saying it would attract business and promote development. Yet South Carolina has long had one of the most regressive tax structures in the nation. If lowering taxes on the rich is the magic bullet to stimulate growth, why has it never worked before?

Creating good public education, infrastructure and cultural amenities is the way civilized states and countries encourage development. But education and infrastructure cost money — money Sanford is not willing to spend if it means raising taxes.

To pay for his income tax cut, Sanford called for a 30-cent-per-pack tax increase on cigarettes. But business and public policy leaders have long called for a tax hike on cigarettes to pay for health care for the state's large uninsured population. Sanford has been opposed to using a cigarette tax to pay for health care for the needy, but he is happy to use it to pay for a tax break for the wealthy.

Anywhere else in the world this would be an outrage. In South Carolina, it's business as usual. It's earned Sanford two terms as governor and — if my hunch is correct — will earn him a run for the White House. And it explains why this woebegone little state always has two wheels in the ditch.

December 14, 2008

(Sanford's flat tax proposal never got off the ground, in part because of the distraction of his "Appalachian Trail" misadventure.)

CUTTING TO THE BONE
STATE BUDGET CUTS ARE MORE THAN AN INCONVENIENCE

When we assess the wreckage that is our state budget, one is left in awestruck wonder at the malfeasance of the people who run this state. Yes, there is a recession, and, yes, all states are feeling the budget crunch. But it didn't have to be this bad.

In an excellent series of stories last week, *The Post and Courier* described the tax-cutting frenzy that set this train wreck in motion.

In 2007, at the same time Gov. Mark Sanford was congratulating the General Assembly for eliminating the residential property tax, John S. Rainey, chairman of the State Board of Economic Advisers, warned that a recession was possible and could come by the beginning of 2008. The state's spending increases and tax cuts could produce "startlingly significant deficits," he reported then.

"That was in everybody's hands in June 2007," he told the *P&C*. "We said, 'If you do nothing else, you'll be short $1 billion in 2010.'"

The crisis arrived two years early. For the last four months we have seen our solons scrambling to cut services to pay for their tax cuts. In fact, the tax cuts of 2006-2007 came to $521 million, according to the *P&C*, and the current budget shortfall stands at $535 million. What a coincidence!

How are these cuts likely to affect the average South Carolinian? Let's take a look at healthcare.

The Medical University of South Carolina has taken a 25 percent budget hit. Twenty-five percent! At MUSC, physicians' training has several sources of funding, but the College of Nursing is funded only by the legislature from the general fund.

When you go to a hospital, who do you think takes care of you? If you are lucky, you will see the doctor for 10 minutes a day. The rest of your care is in the hands of nurses, said Dr. Gail Stuart, dean of the College of Nursing. If you come out of the hospital alive, you might have a nurse to thank. Some 94,000 people a year die in American hospitals due to medical errors.

More nurses mean fewer errors. It's that simple.

"We now have statistics which prove that you have better medical outcomes when you have more nurses on a unit," Stuart said. "Also, the more time a nurse spends with a patient, the better the outcome. And the better educated a nurse, the better the outcome.

"This is not rocket science. Now we have studies to say we know this for sure."

But we will not be getting more nurses in South Carolina because our legislators and governor chose to cut taxes instead; now they are cutting the College of Nursing budget to make ends meet.

As Stuart explained, 93 percent of the operating cost of the College is personnel. There is little else to cut except faculty, and with fewer faculty there can only be fewer nursing graduates, and fewer nurses means less healthcare in South Carolina.

Again, it's that simple. This will not be an inconvenience. It will be a matter of life or death for many — perhaps for you or a member of your family.

What you see happening to our health care is happening across the board — to education, public health, and public safety. In the years to come, we will have fewer Highway Patrol officers on the road and fewer environmental enforcers. The Department of Natural Resources has already started closing field offices; the University of South Carolina may soon be closing three regional campuses. The Department of Education is taking a $253 million cut this year alone.

How will these cuts affect you? In small and unnoticeable ways, for the most part. Such changes are usually incremental. You notice them years later, when you look back and remember how good it used to be. But if you go into a hospital, the results could be immediate and dire. You could be dead.

The fact is that South Carolinians would rather have low taxes than a high quality of life. Or at least the rich would. And it was largely for them that these tax cuts were implemented — especially when it comes to the elimination of residential property taxes.

Of course, the rich can afford private nurses, private schools, private security. The rest of us, well, we will just have to get by. Few will ever understand the connection between our declining quality of life and decisions that were made in Columbia. And the people who run this state like it that way.

January 21, 2009

ADULT SUPERVISION NEEDED
STATE GOVERNMENT LOOKS LIKE SCHOOLYARD BEHAVIOR

In what may be the most misgoverned state in the nation, South Carolina's governor and General Assembly truly outdid themselves this year. Blame it on politics. Blame it on the economy. But don't assume there is any accountable adult willing to stand up and take responsibility.

The nation is in the worst economic downturn in 75 years. While some states are faring better than others, South Carolina is suffering under the third-highest unemployment rate in the country. Yet much of our economic grief was self-inflicted.

South Carolina has a monstrously unbalanced tax system, which relies too much on sales tax. It works well enough when the economy is humming along and everybody is spending freely, but in times like these, there is not enough going into the public coffers, with the result that thousands of state employees get laid off or furloughed. Yet this was a chance the governor and General Assembly were happy to take in 2006, when they overhauled the state tax code to give property tax breaks to some of the richest people in the state. The Strom Thurmond Institute of Government and many others warned that the new tax structure was a disaster waiting to happen. But there were no adults in the Statehouse with the power to rein in this folly.

There should be some satisfaction in knowing that one of the groups that got furloughed was the General Assembly itself. To save money, lawmakers and their staffs were sent home for several weeks over the past legislative session, and a lot of public business did not get done.

But that was only one of the crises the solons had to contend with in 2009. Another was the governor and his overt, opportunistic, intransigent political ambition.

Gov. Mark Sanford — in a performance that has earned him nationwide scorn and the praise of far right-wing Republicans — has refused to accept $700 million in federal stimulus money directed toward education and law enforcement. With the second worst public education system in the nation, hundreds of teachers being laid off across the state, college being priced out of many young people's future, Sanford has chosen to use the issue to elevate his national profile and his 2012 presidential prospects.

The rift between Sanford and the leaders of his own party over taking federal stimulus money has gone from ugly to vicious. Senate Majority Leader Glenn McConnell and House Speaker Bobby Harrell have publicly torn into Sanford.

In a guest column that Harrell wrote for *The State*, he said that Sanford "is in essence telling our citizens who have no bread to just eat cake instead."

McConnell's open letter to the governor, published in *The Post and Courier*, said, "Time and again, you have failed to address problems in a constructive manner and proactively work with the Legislature to find solutions. For seven years now, on issue after issue, you have chosen to make headlines rather than to make headway and to create problems rather than to solve them."

Last week the General Assembly passed legislation requiring Sanford to take the stimulus money. The governor responded with a lawsuit, saying the Legislature's actions would have "far-reaching implications for future governors."

Excuse me, but I thought all true conservatives hated the courts for thwarting popular will and overturning the laws of state and federal legislatures. So much for "strict constructionism." And one more thing: Who's paying for this lawsuit anyway?

As this legal drama plays out in the final days of the legislative session, we are treated to the annual sight of Sanford vetoing dozens of budget items, only to have the legislators override said vetoes with the speed and efficiency of Burger King.

In the midst of this rancor and the abbreviated legislative session, key bills did not make it through the General Assembly. That is good news and bad news.

The good news is that bills authorizing voter ID, school vouchers, and a 24-hour abortion waiting period ran out of time. The bad news is that time also ran out on a cigarette tax increase. This was to be the year that we finally raise the cigarette tax from seven cents a pack — the nation's lowest — and use the 50 cent increase to fund health care for the poor. Too bad it didn't pass. And the poor probably got screwed again when the Legislature passed a weak and watered-down last-minute bill to curb the abuses of payday lenders. This predatory industry should be put out of the state, not rapped on the knuckles.

Here's my suggestion: Let's send the General Assembly to time-out until January and sit Gov. Sanford in the corner with a dunce cap.

May 27, 2009

(Sanford finally accepted the federal stimulus money after the state Supreme Court rejected his suit.)

THE GREATEST STORY SINCE SECESSION
HOW CAN SUCH A LITTLE STATE BE SO ENTERTAINING?

How quickly things change. I had already written three-quarters of a column last week about the unfolding events at the Statehouse. It took the form of a satirical open letter to Gov. Mark Sanford, commiserating with him about the pressures of work and the need to get away from it all from time to time. In less than 12 hours the governor's alleged Appalachian Trail hike had turned from whimsical misadventure into a tragedy of near-Shakespearean proportions.

Among those trying to repair his damaged reputation is your humble correspondent. Barely an hour before the news conference in which our governor committed political hara-kiri with his announcement of an extramarital affair, I was having lunch with an out-of-state friend, explaining that whatever the governor was up to, it had nothing to do with women, booze, or drugs. "He's a straight arrow," I told her. "He lacks the imagination for an affair."

Now you know why I never made the major leagues of political analysis.

Of course, I was the least of Mark Sanford's victims. Among the greatest was Sanford's wife, Jenny. She managed his first gubernatorial campaign out of their house in 2002, even as she managed the house and their four sons, and she was widely credited with helping to engineer the primary defeat of Sen. John Kuhn, a Charleston Republican and one of her husband's sharpest critics, in 2004. And for nearly 20 years, some might say, the industrial heiress has been not only his confidante and aide, but his meal ticket. This is her reward?

In his statement to a packed and hungry press gallery at the Statehouse, Sanford said last week that his wife had known about the "relationship" with an unidentified Argentine woman for five months, and in that time he and his wife had been trying to "work through" this painful situation.

Five months. That almost exactly corresponds with the surreal period in which our governor very loudly and piously refused to accept $700 million in federal stimulus funds directed at state schools and law enforcement. In the face of the second-highest unemployment rate in the nation and brutal criticism from leaders of his own party, Sanford insisted that any stimulus money must be used to pay down state debt. When the General Assembly passed legislation forcing him to accept the money, he went to the state Supreme Court, where he lost the battle and finally surrendered.

Throughout the protracted dispute, there was something unsettling and almost maniacal about Sanford's self-righteousness and his dismissal of all criticism. Now we learn that this public drama was playing out at the same time the private drama of his failing marriage was unfolding off stage. I leave it to his shrink to explain the dynamics of that duality, but I find it rather frightening. And this guy was grooming himself for the presidency!

Now it's just a question of what Mark Sanford should do next. At the news conference last Wednesday, he refused to answer a question about whether he would resign. My question would be — what else can he do?

Sanford has never had an effective working relationship with the General Assembly. His gubernatorial tenure has been a constant train of name-calling and finger-pointing, of vetoes and veto-overrides. But he possessed a populist appeal, based on his image as a maverick and man of principle. Now that is gone, along with any moral authority to govern.

And his current behavior brings his past record into high profile. As a member of the U.S. House of Representatives, he voted to impeach President Bill Clinton in 1998, in connection with the Monica Lewinsky scandal.

"I think it would be much better for the country and for him personally (to resign)," Sanford said during the impeachment debate. "I come from the business side ... If you had a chairman or president in the business world facing these allegations, he'd be gone."

What allegations? That Clinton had an affair or that he lied to cover it up? It doesn't matter in Sanford's case, because he is guilty of both, having told his staff that he was hiking the Appalachian Trail when he was, in fact, flying to Argentina to meet his mistress.

Of course, the greatest victim of this fraud has been the people of South Carolina. They were gulled by yet another charlatan who violated their trust and embarrassed them on CNN.

Did they learn anything? Of course not! They will give their votes to the next smooth-talking huckster who knows how to use the code words of white identity and Christian evangelism. And to look at the host of GOP candidates lining up for the job, they will have plenty to chose from.

July 1, 2009

(Actually, they gave their votes to Mark Sanford again, electing in to his old First District U.S. House seat in 2013.)

THE OLD SHELL GAME
LEGISLATURE KEEPS US DISTRACTED AND BAMBOOZLED

You know the General Assembly is ready to convene for its 2010 session when legislators start pre-filing bills, and you have that sinking feeling that when they go home in June not a damned thing is going to be better for this god-forsaken state. Our legislators will do anything to distract themselves, to distract the public, to pretend to be doing something to earn another term in Columbia. The artifice of governance goes on, year after year, and we never figure out which shell the pea is hiding under — and that it doesn't matter anyway.

Charleston Rep. Wendell Gilliard has a reputation for grandstanding and making much ado over little. His latest stunt is perhaps his craziest. (I will resist the obvious pun which this story so richly deserves.) He wants to allow guests at Charlestowne Landing and other state parks to be able to collect pecans for five dollars a bag and then apply that fee toward the general budget. Of course, that budget got cut by hundreds of millions of dollars this past year. Does Gilliard really think he is solving a problem with this hare-brained fund-raising scheme?

If that idea is silly, Sen. Chip Campsen's bill is downright insidious — insidious because it will allow our lawmakers and the public a smug sense of self-satisfaction, while doing almost nothing to protect the most vulnerable members of society.

Campsen wants to ban registered sex offenders from Internet social networking sites for the purpose of protecting underage children from sexual predators. The bill, patterned after one in New York State, involves turning names of registered sex offenders over to social network managers, who then cancel their accounts.

Worthy goal, to be sure, and you really must admire Campsen for standing up to the sexual predator lobby and saying, We've had enough! And I have no doubt that our courageous General Assembly will fall in behind the senator from Mt. Pleasant in telling sexual predators that our children are off limits. The *Post and Courier* has even gotten into this crusade with a recent column by editor emeritus Barbara Williams. Yes, she's against sexual predators, too!

After this law is passed — as I am sure it will be — I wonder what new steps our fearless leaders will take to make South Carolina children safe. They will certainly have their work cut out for them.

South Carolina has one of the highest teen smoking rates in the nation, yet spends less than any other state on programs to prevent children from using tobacco. South Carolina ranks eighth in the nation in teen birthrate; not surprising since our lawmakers would rather give sexually active teens Jesus than reliable sex education.

The number of South Carolina students eligible for free and reduced-price meals ranks second-highest in the nation. In fact, the Palmetto State was recently number one for the number of households with people who go without food, according to the U.S. Department of Agriculture. That's a lot of children going to school hungry.

In other surveys, South Carolina students rank 49th or 50th annually in SAT scores. We had the highest school dropout rate in the nation and ranked 41st in overall achievement, based on test scores related to reading and math performance, high school graduation rates, and Advanced Placement exams.

In the annual report from the Every Child Matters Education Fund, South Carolina ranked 45th in the nation on overall child well-being. The ranking was based on 10 criteria, including infant death rate, death rate of older children, births to teen mothers, births to women receiving late or no prenatal care, children living in poverty, uninsured children, juvenile incarceration rates, child abuse fatalities, and per capita child welfare expenditures. Nowhere did the study factor in the threat of sexual predators on the internet — the great danger that seems to keep Chip Campsen and Barbara Williams awake at night.

Another irony in Campsen's bill is that children cannot encounter sexual predators online if they do not have a computer, and South Carolina ranks 44th in the nation for internet access in the home. Slightly less than 60 percent of South Carolina homes had access last year, according to the U.S. Census Bureau. Computer access in South Carolina public schools is also among the lowest in the nation.

Wouldn't it be wonderful if Campsen were as worried about providing online access as he is about dirty old men hanging out on social networking sites? But he probably considers lack of access to be a way of protecting children from predators.

With leadership like Gilliard's and Campsen's, I am confident we will soon feel much better about our budget and the future of our children.

January 13, 2010

MORTGAGING OUR FUTURE
OUR LEADERS ALWAYS LIKED THE PAST BETTER ANYWAY

So much of what is wrong with South Carolina's politics, economy, and society was on vivid display last week in two big news stories.

First, on Sunday, *The Post and Courier* reported that college tuition rates in South Carolina's state-supported colleges were the highest in the Southeast. The cost of a four-year university degree has tripled in this state over the last decade. The *P&C* story singled out the College of Charleston as "this year's poster child for tuition increases with an eye-popping 14.8 percent increase to in-state rates." At the current rate of increase, an 8-year-old today would need $120,000 for in-state tuition in 2020, according to the *P&C* story.

The reasons for the rate hikes are complex, and there is plenty of blame to go around. But most of it must be placed at the door of the General Assembly.

Funding for our state colleges and universities has simply not kept up. In fact, it has declined over the past decade. Of course, the entire state budget has taken a beating in recent years, but there is something particularly fatalistic about cutting funding for public schools and colleges.

As politicians love to tell us, "Our children are our future." It is one of the few things you will ever hear a politician say that is so clearly and so startlingly true. However, our elected officials in Columbia would rather defund that future.

The reason the states — including South Carolina — got into public education and public colleges in the 19th century was to make education available to a broad segment of the public. It was an early and important step in the democratization of the young Republic, a step that was quite late in coming to the South.

In other regions of the country, it was argued that educated people made better citizens and better voters. That argument never held much water in the South, where voting rights were limited to a narrow demographic of land-owning white males and citizenship, as a concept, was pretty much limited to the same.

Then, after World War II, the push came for broad economic development in the South and the value of education took on new meaning. An educated workforce was needed both for line production and for management. If we wanted a better future, we needed better schools and colleges. It was that simple, and South Carolina invested seriously in education from the 1950s into the '80s. But today education is treated more like state parks and highway rest stops — as a budgetary item that is dispensable in tough times.

Only 22 percent of South Carolina adults have bachelor's degrees, ranking us 39th in the nation. And some people in Columbia seem to think that's good enough. Yet one thing is certain: As the price of a college education goes out of reach for more and more middle-class folk, the wealthy will always be able to educate their children. And as they do, South Carolina will begin to look more and more like the feudal society it was in the nineteenth century.

I think some people in Columbia would be quite comfortable with that. They have always believed they were there to serve wealth and power, and shrinking the educated middle class would be a good way to do that in a contracting economy.

The other piece of information that made this picture complete arrived Wednesday, when *The State* newspaper reported that Republican gubernatorial candidate Nikki Haley wants to do away with the state's corporate income tax. She calls it "job creation."

Scrapping the corporate income tax has been a Republican dream for years. (The proposal is further proof that Haley is just Mark Sanford in lipstick.) South Carolina already has the 37th lowest tax structure in the nation. If low taxes were all that was needed to attract jobs and industry, this state would be developed from the mountains to the coast. But in fact, when corporate scouts go looking for a site for a new factory or headquarters, they are looking for more than low taxes. They are looking for an educated workforce. They are looking for good schools and affordable colleges and universities for their children. They are looking for modern, dependable infrastructure. And they want the kind of cultural and recreational amenities that only tax dollars can pay for.

You won't get any of those things by cutting corporate taxes, Nikki. But, of course, you will please your friends and supporters immensely, and that's really what it's all about, isn't it?

Making college unaffordable to the middle class and rewarding the wealthy, with corporate tax cuts: It sounds like a perfect formula for driving this state back to the nineteenth century.

August 18, 2010

STATE OF MIND
FEUDALISM LIVES IN SOUTH CAROLINA

"Who's that?"
"I dunno. Must be a king."
"Why?"
"He hasn't got shit all over him."

— from "Monty Python and the Holy Grail"

Ah, the Middle Ages. Those were the days. Life was so much simpler then.

For one thing, everyone knew his place and stayed in it. And it was so easy to tell the kings from everyone else in those old feudal times. The king — and a few of his friends and family — didn't have shit all over them. And everyone else did. That's all you had to know.

Leave it to the South Carolina Republican Party to bring back those good old times. They have been working at it for years by giving us one of the most regressive tax codes in the nation.

They scored a huge breakthrough when they herded the General Assembly into doing away with taxes on most residential properties in 2007. The legislature eliminated the school operations portion of the property tax and capped reassessment at 15 percent for residential properties that had not changed hands. The lost revenue would be offset by a small increase in the sales tax. And to those who cried that the sales tax is regressive and falls disproportionately on the poor and middle class, the tax reformers threw us a bone: eliminating the tax on most groceries. The average household saved about $218 a year on that little benevolence. Wealthy property owners saved thousands on the property tax overhaul.

From the beginning, critics screamed that it wouldn't work. The marginal sales tax increase could never replace lost property tax.

Today, those Cassandras have been proven right. South Carolina's schools are in desperate straights as teachers are laid off and furloughed, class sizes swell, and extracurricular programs are cut.

Currently, the state Tax Realignment Commission is studying ways to increase revenue without inconveniencing the wealthy. One option they are looking at would raise the sales tax on groceries back to their pre-2007 levels or higher. Other options on the table include taxing prescription drugs, water, and electric power, three things that have never been taxed in this state before. Yes, in a state where hundreds of our poorest residents have sought relief in paying their power bills during this scorching season, there are powerful individuals in Columbia who want to raise their power bills with a new tax.

GOP gubernatorial candidate Nikki Haley has demonstrated that she is on board with the TRC's feed-the-rich agenda. She wants to raise the sales tax on groceries and eliminate the corporate income tax.

More taxes on the working class and the middle class — this is the price we may soon pay to protect the feudal prerogatives of this state's ruling class. Think I exaggerate?

The man who led the statewide campaign to abolish property tax in 2007 is a local millionaire named Emerson Read Sr. Though he did not completely succeed in his goal, his friends thought he had come close enough to merit special recognition. In October of that year, the French Society of Charleston met at the Carolina

Yacht Club for their 191st anniversary dinner. There, men in white ties and tails and women in evening gowns applauded enthusiastically as Read received the Society's Humanitati Award in recognition of his efforts to "improve the human condition either in his community or the world at large."

"Like a savior, he was there when we needed him," French Society member Jack Simmons told the yacht club crowd. "And by 'we' I mean every single South Carolinian and potentially every United States citizen."

That's right! The ruling class of South Carolina considers that cutting their property taxes was nothing less than a great humanitarian triumph. Furthermore, they think they speak for "every single South Carolinian and ... every United States citizen."

Cloaked in such self-delusion, the plutocrats of this state make no apology for ruling over us with something like divine right. After all, they have been doing it for more than 300 years. Those wealthy bastards think we should be grateful for their wisdom and benefactions.

I have written here before that the people who run this state consider it their job to serve wealth and power. It is a medieval concept that came here on the first ships that entered Charleston harbor in 1670, and we have never gotten over it.

It's downright feudal in its implications for working-class and middle-class people. And it means we're about to get covered with shit again. And again. And again.

August 25, 2010

DOWN THE HOLE
SOUTH CAROLINA FLUSHES ITS FUTURE AWAY

If South Carolina is famous for anything, it is the willingness to draw a line in the sand, to tell the world "enough is enough," to push back when we feel outsiders impinging upon our sovereignty. We stood up to the Lord's Proprietors in 1718. We put the British out in 1776, and when they captured Charleston in 1780, we put them out again. And I don't have to remind you what happened in 1860. We have demonstrated that we will face any foe and pay any price to defend our state's honor. Honor means a lot to South Carolinians.

But for all our pugnacity in dealing with outsiders, we have shown a sad lack of courage in dealing with our own inner demons — and there are many.

Right now this state faces a budget crisis of historic proportions. It is not unreasonable to say that the way we live now and for generations to come is at stake. As we go into the third year of economic decline, the state is facing an $800 million budget shortfall. And that is on top of nearly $2 billion in budget cuts over the last two years.

According to the Associated Press, the bulk of the cutting will come to those programs that aid the poor, the young, the elderly.

Education? Our lawmakers are talking about cutting 10 days out of the school year in a state that already has one of the lowest performing school systems in the nation. So much for all those years of bold talk about making South Carolina's schools competitive.

Healthcare? The state's Medicaid system, which provides for the poor and indigent, faces a $228 million deficit.

Nourishment? The Department of Social Services has cut staff by 14 percent, even as food stamp demand is up 51 percent and demand for temporary financial assistance is up 44 percent.

Environmental quality? The Department of Health and Environmental Control no longer has the manpower to adequately monitor public waterways for mercury and PCBs.

Make no mistake, the budget crisis — and the way our leaders have chosen to face it — represents a major retreat from the challenges that face our state. A retreat from education standards. A retreat from a clean and safe environment. A retreat from the dream of adequate food and medical care for the most vulnerable. A retreat from our dreams of becoming a socially and economically developed state, competitive with other states in something other than football and baseball.

This budget represents a withdrawal, a turning in upon ourselves, a shrinking of our hopes and aspirations. We are burning the bulkheads to roast our marshmallows, because without a healthy, educated population, we do not have the raw material for development.

Will outside investors come here to build their factories and hire our people, as GOPers are so fond of saying? Sure, they will go anywhere with low wages and environmental standards. Just ask a Mexican or Malaysian. They will build their factories here all right. And they will import their skilled workers, live in gated communities, send their children to private schools, have their private security force, and maybe even have their own water, sewer, and electric services. And they will hire us to mow their lawns and cook their meals, because we will not be qualified to do anything else.

Those who are old enough may some day remember that things used to be different. There used to be hope. There used to be talk of better schools, better jobs, better days to come. And they may remember that in the Great Recession of the early twenty-first century, our leaders surrendered to fear and greed.

They may remember that we did not draw a line in the sand. We did not say we will stand up, we will do whatever it takes to save our state, our environment, our way of life. We did not say it was a matter of honor that we protect and educate our young, that we care for our most vulnerable.

It doesn't have to be that way, of course. Our leaders might ask us — especially the most prosperous among us — to reach a little deeper in our pockets to support the services and agencies that keep this state functioning as a modern society. But in this crisis, Gov.-elect Nikki Haley promises to do away with corporate income taxes.

Of course, Republicans will argue that lower taxes stimulate growth. But in a state with some of the lowest taxes in the nation, why is our economy in the toilet? Today, with the lowest federal taxes in 60 years, why is the nation's economy going down the crapper?

And if you ask a GOPer what that whooshing noise is, he would probably tell you it's the sound of progress and prosperity sweeping us forward. He would be wrong.

December 8, 2010

BACK ON THE JOB
THE GENERAL ASSEMBLY RESUMES ITS MISRULE IN COLUMBIA

It's not easy to know whether our state Legislature is just plain stupid, or if there's something deeper — a genuine, intrinsic malevolence.

With regard to our current budget crisis, it's easy to believe we are looking at stupidity. Four years ago, the Republican General Assembly gave huge property tax rollbacks to some of the wealthiest residents — and biggest campaign donors — in the state. They sought to make up the difference with a hike in the sales tax. They did this even as economic advisers and tax experts warned that this was folly, that when the economy slowed down, sales tax revenues would tank.

That's exactly what has happened as South Carolina wallows in the deepest economic crisis since the Great Depression. Today the state faces an $829 million budget shortfall, and this after the budget already has been slashed by $2 billion over the last two years. There is pain throughout the land as agencies reduce services, close offices, furlough workers, cut Medicaid, and even contemplate trimming 10 days off the school year.

One suspects that this is gross stupidity. After all, the anger and anguish of this poor state is aimed directly at the General Assembly. Our solons look helpless and witless, and we know that was never their intention, for they are nothing if not vain. They played with fire, and they got burned — along with the rest of us.

Yes, we can mark that one up to stupidity. But the economy is not the only crisis in our state. We have a crisis of democracy, as exemplified by our broken election system. We saw this all too vividly in the Democratic primary last June, the primary in which an unemployed man who had never sought public office, who did not have a campaign staff or an office or even a computer, defeated a seasoned and well-funded political figure who had been campaigning around the state for months.

There has never been a credible explanation for Alvin Greene's 20-percent victory margin over Vic Rawl. Cynicism about the Democratic primary was inevitable in light of several well-publicized technical and human failures since the iVotronic machines were purchased in 2004 to serve all 46 counties. Most recently, there were at least two major snafus in the 2010 general election.

In November, Colleton County reported 13,045 votes for statewide offices, though only 11,656 ballots were cast. The problem stemmed from voting machines counting 1,389 votes twice, an acknowledged problem with these machines.

In Lancaster County last fall, a Freedom of Information Act request revealed that the usual digital files resulting from an election did not in fact exist. Totaling the votes was done manually. There was a discrepancy between the database at county headquarters and the databases in the individual machines, making the automatic aggregation of votes from individual machines impossible.

These are just a couple of the problems with the iVotronic machines in recent years. In other cases, miscalibrated machines resulted in names lighting up on the touch screen that voters had not selected. Dr. Duncan Buell, chairman of the University of South Carolina Department of Computer Science and Engineering, has warned that the state's voting machines can be hacked.

There is one solution that would solve almost all the voting machine problems and go a long way toward restoring public faith in the electoral process: have the machines issue a printed record to each voter of the ballot he just cast.

"We have no ability in South Carolina to count anything except what gets stored in the memory chips of the voting machines," Buell told a Spartanburg TV station. "There is no paper record."

It just happens that there are several pieces of legislation dealing with election law that have been prefiled as the General Assembly returns to begin its 2011 session. Unfortunately, giving our voting machines a paper record is not one of them.

No, our GOP Legislature is intent on passing laws to reduce opportunities for absentee voting and forcing voters to produce a photo ID to cast a ballot, even when they have a voter registration card. Research shows that all of these measures have the effect of suppressing the vote, and those most often disenfranchised are the poor and the elderly. Why do the GOPers want to push through these changes in the state's election law? They say it is to prevent voter fraud, yet there have been no cases of voter fraud recorded in the state in decades.

With all the election problems we face in this state, the GOPers are intent on solving a problem that does not exist, even as they disenfranchise thousands of voters in the state. That, my friends, is not stupidity. That is malevolence.

January 19, 2011

(Voting machines in South Carolina still offer no paper record of a voter's choice; a watered-down version of voter ID went into effect in January 2013.).

STATE OF DENIAL
SOUTH CAROLINA DENIES ITS WORKERS DIGNITY AND SAFETY

If you have never heard of Workers Memorial Day, you are not alone. I had never heard of it either until last week. That was when I read the story in *The Post and Courier* about Tina and David Williamson, who lost their 18-year-old son Matthew six years ago in an accident at Detyens Shipyard, in North Charleston.

"I felt like my son had been murdered because of the way he had been taken from me," Tina Williamson said in that story. Last week, she organized a candlelight vigil in Summerville for the friends and loved ones of workers who have died on the job.

The day of the vigil was April 28, Workers Memorial Day. The date was chosen because it is the anniversary of 1971's Occupational Safety and Health Act. The first Workers Memorial Day was observed in 1989. Every year, people in hundreds of communities and workplaces around the country recognize those workers who are killed or injured on the job. The day is recognized by national governments in scores of countries, including the U.S., and a number of states. It is observed by trade unions around the world. In 2001, the United Nations recognized Workers Memorial Day, declaring it World Day for Safety and Health at Work.

Of course, few in the Palmetto State have ever heard of Workers Memorial Day. After all, this state has had a long and ugly relationship with its workforce. You probably have heard of South Carolina's first workers. They were called slaves — and you know how that ended. Things didn't get much better for workers after the Civil War. Any attempt to organize or create unions or cooperative stores was met in much the same way as slave rebellions of the past — by police, militia, mob violence, or some combination of the three.

State and municipal governments and law enforcement were universally allied with employers to maintain order and keep dissidents out. Events came to a tragic head in Honea Path during the Great Textile Strike of 1934, when a specially deputized mob of

125 men fired on striking workers in front of Chiquola Mill. Seven workers were killed, and some 30 injured. Dan Beacham, the man who deputized the gunmen, was the mayor of Honea Path and the superintendent of Chiquola Mill.

In recent weeks, Gov. Nikki Haley's anti-union rhetoric prompted a lawsuit by the AFL-CIO and the National Labor Relations Board. Two weeks ago, Haley, Mayor Joseph P. Riley Jr., Sen. Lindsey Graham, and other politicos stood shoulder-to-shoulder at a press conference in North Charleston to declare that they intended to keep unions out of the new Boeing plant under construction in North Charleston and to keep South Carolina a right-to-work state.

This is the history of labor in South Carolina. Less than five percent of this state's workforce is organized, and powerful forces are working to reduce that number. So it is not surprising that Workers Memorial Day has never gotten much traction here. But that very fact demonstrates how much we need strong unions in South Carolina and throughout the nation.

In 2009 (the latest figures available), 4,340 workers were killed on the job in the U.S., an average of 12 workers a day. An estimated 50,000 died of occupational diseases. More than 4.1 million workplace injuries and illnesses were reported in private, state, and municipal workplaces, according to the AFL-CIO.

Last year's string of major workplace tragedies demonstrates the need for stronger safety and health rules, coupled with tougher enforcement. Those disasters included the Upper Big Branch Mine explosion, which killed 29 miners in West Virginia; an explosion at the Kleen Energy plant in Middletown, Conn., which killed six workers; another at the Tesoro Refinery in Washington state, which killed seven workers; and the BP/Deepwater Horizon Gulf Coast oil rig explosion, which killed 11 and caused a massive environmental and economic disaster.

In South Carolina, attempts to have the governor or General Assembly recognize Workers Memorial Day have failed. No effort was made this year. But the fact is that union workers get better training, which makes them safer workers, and most union workers take advantage of OSHA classes that unions provide at no cost, says Erin McKee, president of the Greater Charleston Labor Council. And with a union contract they are not afraid to speak out as nonunion workers are.

Those who work with their hands have never been respected in this state. Just as it is popular to deny the role of slavery in launching the Civil War, so it is also popular in wide circles to deny the role of labor in building our state and our nation. And even though scores of these workers die in South Carolina each year, the people who run our state government deny them a day of recognition.

May 4, 2011

TRADITION OVER EDUCATION
MICK ZAIS PLAYS ONE TO THE GRANDSTANDS

The Palmetto State Pathology has many symptoms: poor public education, low personal income, and high rates of poverty, crime, divorce, infant mortality, and violence toward women and children, among other things. But all of these symptoms have one origin: a world view among the majority of the white population focused on past fears and resentments, and incapable of facing the world as it is rather than the way it was or might have been.

We saw a stunning example of this old way of thinking recently when state Superintendent of Education Mick Zais unilaterally took South Carolina out of the running for up to $50 million in federal grant money for public schools. That $50 million is part of a $200 million pot of money the U.S. Department of Education is handing out to help reform some of the lowest-performing state school systems in the country. South Carolina certainly qualifies.

The money is allocated under a federal education program called Race to the Top. The state applied for one of the Race to the Top grants under previous state Superintendent Jim Rex, a

Democrat. Zais, a Republican, campaigned last year against South Carolina's participation in the Race to the Top program. The white people of the state elected him, and Zais made good on his promise. He walked away from millions of dollars that might have supported teachers, schools, and students in this woebegone state.

People outside South Carolina probably have a hard time understanding this decision, but I suspect it is popular enough among Zais' supporters. It hearkens back to the day two years ago when then-Gov. Mark Sanford tried to reject $700 million in federal stimulus money, even as the state floundered in 10 percent unemployment.

Zais justified his decision, saying that taking federal education money was tantamount to taking "pieces of silver in exchange for strings attached to Washington." This is strange logic, indeed, coming from a retired Army general who spent his career taking orders from Washington. Zais' career also includes a short stint as president of tiny Newberry College in the Upstate. His resumé does not reflect any experience in public education.

By contrast, his Democratic opponent in last fall's election was Frank Holleman, a Greenville attorney who served as the deputy U.S. secretary of education and helped found the state's First Steps to School Readiness program.

Also at the national level, he worked in the Government Accountability Office's Expert Panel for K-12 Education and was a member of the federal Advisory Committee on Student Financial Assistance. Holleman understood the value of good connections in Washington.

Holleman has called Greenville his home for more than 30 years. He and his wife are graduates of Furman University, and his children are products of South Carolina public schools. Yet during the fall campaign, his opponents turned his experience against him. In true South Carolina form, they cited his "years in Washington" as a point of suspicion. (Years of experience in Washington never seems to diminish the appeal of Republican politicians. See: Thurmond, Strom.)

What Zais did with the Race to the Top funds was cynical beyond words, yet it is what white politicians have done in this state for generations. When it is convenient, they will readily disparage federal money as corrupt and manipulative. It is a charade that dates back at least to the New Deal, and it elicits strains of pride among whites, who still revere the idea of secession and belligerence toward the federal government.

I call it a charade because the same politicians who spend their careers denouncing and denigrating everything that emanates from the national capital would dance on their Confederate granddaddy's grave for the opportunity to go to Congress. And white voters who support those politicians who spurn federal stimulus and education money will revere another politician who "brings home the bacon" to build a popular road, airport, or bridge (See: Ravenel, Arthur)

And Zais' cynicism has an even darker side. Sure, many white voters will support him for turning down that evil federal money, but the money was intended to help children, and children don't vote. Zais pulled a grandstand play with little downside, and I am sure he will remind his white supporters of it at the next election.

What were the federal "strings" that were so onerous that they made tens of millions of dollars unpalatable to the superintendent of education? He didn't specify, but it is hard to believe that running schools the Washington way could be any worse than the way we have been doing it for the last 140 years.

As Andy Brack of the *Statehouse Report* wrote: "Maybe we need these so-called government strings. Why? Because what's been happening so far with us at the bottom of education lists hasn't been working out that well."

But that's tradition, and in the Palmetto State, tradition trumps all.

June 8, 2011

NIKKI AND KEN
WHO WILL BE THE FIRST TO DO THE PERP WALK?

How much longer can Nikki Haley's luck hold out? Not only did she come out of nowhere to become governor in 2010, she did it despite having two men with sworn affidavits claiming to have had extramarital affairs with her. And she did it despite serious questions about her personal finances, her employment record, and her personal veracity.

Once elected, she continued to stumble. First, she removed Darla Moore from the University of South Carolina Board of Trustees. Moore is the greatest benefactor in the history of USC, having donated tens of millions of dollars of personal wealth to the institution. Haley replaced Moore with one of her campaign contributors.

Now, she is being called onto the carpet by Democrats and some in the media over the way she left Columbia for a trip to New York last month. The timing was particularly awkward. A few weeks earlier she had insisted that the General Assembly stay in Columbia to finish its budget and other business. But on June 29, she left town to attend the Republican Governor's Association meeting. The Legislature was still in session dealing with her budget vetoes, and there was certainly the appearance that she was setting one standard for the Legislature and another for herself.

Last week, media outlets reported that she was doing more than hobnobbing with the GOPer guvs and spending personal time with her family, as her staff reported. She attended a fundraiser where she picked up $32,000, mostly from out-of-state donors, for her re-election campaign.

Haley did nothing illegal by removing Moore from the USC board or failing to disclose her hidden agenda in leaving Columbia for the Big Apple while the General Assembly was still in session. But it does raise questions as to her judgment and priorities.

In a recent story in *The Nation*, *Columbia Free Times* reporter and *City Paper* contributor Corey Hutchins raised far more troubling questions.

"I believe she is the most corrupt person to occupy the governor's mansion since Reconstruction," John Rainey, a longtime Republican fundraiser and power broker, told Hutchins. "I do not know of any person who ran for governor in my lifetime with as many charges against him or her as she has had that went unanswered."

Among other things, Hutchins cited Haley's record of appointing cronies, fundraisers, and political supporters to key state positions, including the director of her Board of Economic Advisers. She also created a highly paid new position for the wife of her highly paid chief of staff, Tim Pearson. She has also taken on a dollar-a-year staffer, Christian Soura, whose primary salary comes from a right-wing think tank, the S.C. Center for Transforming Government. While Soura has access to state government, the think tank does not have to disclose anything about its finances or operations.

Hutchins rehashes stories of her questionable consulting job while she served as a legislator, as well as her late IRS filings. "More curious," Hutchins writes, "in 2006 Haley and her husband, Michael, claimed only $40,269 in combined income. This was while the couple was paying a $289,000 mortgage, driving a luxury SUV, and raising two children."

Here is my question? What if Nikki Haley suddenly found herself under state or federal criminal investigation or indictment? Is Lt. Gov. Ken Ard ready to step up and assume the office of governor?

Recent revelations about Ard suggest not. He may be too busy talking to his own lawyers.

Since the November election, a flood of reports have shown how truly stupid and irresponsible this former Florence County councilman is. I use the words "stupid" and "irresponsible" because his defenders insist he is too honest to be the weasel he appears to be.

After the election, Ard went on a spending spree, tapping into unspent campaign donations to buy a $3,000 flat-screen TV, iPads, a PlayStation, tickets to the SEC championship game in Atlanta (where he watched Auburn throttle the Gamecocks), and a family vacation. Perhaps even worse, when investigators started asking questions about his behavior, he apparently lied — twice — about his motives and other details. The State Ethics Commission has hit him with $48,400 in fines and ordered him to reimburse the commission $12,500 for the investigation.

All of this comes less than two years after former Gov. Mark Sanford humiliated himself with an Argentine mistress and got hit with more than $70,000 in Ethics Commission fines for various misdeeds.

My last question is this: Why do the people of South Carolina keep embarrassing themselves and the state by electing such people to high office? I think it has something to do with the sense of entitlement that many GOPers attach to holding public office. Whatever the reason, I predict that we are in for another round of bashing by the late night comics. Jon Stewart loves us.

July 20, 2011

(In March 2012, Ken Ard resigned the lieutenant governor's office and pleaded guilty to seven counts of violating the State Ethics Act. He was sentenced five years probation, a $5,000 fine and 300 hours of community service.)

LIBERTARIANISM OR IGNORANCE?
IT'S HARD TO TELL THEM APART AT THE BALLOT BOX

I was recently approaching a bridge over one of our local waterways when I realized it had just been closed. The line of cars came dutifully to a stop, facing the fire truck that blocked the lane.

Turns out there was a wreck that had to be cleared, and it was going to take a long time. Motorists got out of their cars, trucks, and SUVs and started mingling on the roadside, as if at a cocktail party. I heard small talk, speculation, and stories about other wrecks and bridge closings and the worsening traffic in the Lowcountry.

A middle-aged lady in a T-shirt with an invitation to attend her church started talking to me about a recent road closing she had encountered. Seems a limb had fallen from one of our majestic live oaks and obstructed some suburban thoroughfare. The authorities quickly took control of the scene, she said, and wouldn't let anyone approach the fallen limb. Only the designated city work crew could do the job. When they finally arrived, it took them too long to saw the limb into small pieces — much too small, according to the church lady — and finally open the road for passage.

She concluded her little parable with this: "Anybody could have brought their saw and removed that limb, but the city had to do it. That's what happens whenever the government gets involved. They just make a mess of everything."

It was the kind of homegrown homily you might hear at most barbershops or bars in this part of the country. Distrust of government — any government — runs deep in the local DNA. The church lady had performed a little social ritual that Southerners – especially white Southerners – like to share with each other.

It's a gesture people use to bond and to check each other out. And, in fact, some of the Bubbas in our roadside circle nodded and grunted their approval. I walked away.

A half-century ago these rituals had a decidedly more pathological cast. Two or more white men could hardly gather to discuss anything without one of them making some offhanded joke or menacing remark about African Americans. Anyone who did not show proper appreciation might find himself being watched and whispered about. This is what political correctness used to look like.

Today much of that overt hostility has been transferred from black people to the "gubmint." Of course, this is at least in part because it was federal government — in the form of court decisions and civil rights legislation — that came to the defense of black people in the South. This was an invasion of states' rights that many white people have never forgiven. But some of this hostility toward government comes from a deep streak of Southern libertarianism.

This libertarianism expresses itself in a number of ways. One is an antipathy to environmental regulation, which often plays out as hostility toward the environment. You can see this in the stunning number of conservatives who dismiss the threats of global climate change in the face of overwhelming evidence. And then there was the North Carolina man a few years ago who took a chainsaw to the trees on his property rather than have them protected by a new ordinance. Another manifestation of libertarianism is a strong anti-union sentiment. Many Southerners would rather be screwed over by their employers in a "free market" than join a union or be protected by federal labor laws. They forget, of course, that it was unions and the federal government that gave them the 40-hour week, minimum wage, time-and-a-half pay, and myriad other protections and benefits. Old mental habits die hard.

The general hostility that many conservatives — especially white Southerners — feel toward the federal government is expressed by Texas governor and presidential candidate Rick Perry when he says, "I want to make the federal government as inconsequential as possible in your life." But how consequential is government in our lives compared to the power of that other great American entity: the corporation?

We are affected much more by corporations than by government. Ever been screwed by a credit card company, an insurance company, or a bank? Don't complain to the Better Business Bureau. Only the government — state or federal — has the power and the interest to step in for you. It's the government that protects our food from contamination, protects our markets from financial predators, protects the air we breathe and the water we drink from those who would foul them for profit.

Yet, with the short-sightedness of a Walmart Republican, many people insist corporations are their friends and government is the enemy. Whether this is an expression of libertarianism or ignorance, the effect is the same — a society friendly to corporations and hostile to people and the environment.

September 11, 2011

SOUTH CAROLINA BY THE NUMBERS
THEY ADD UP TO A VERY TROUBLED STATE

For years I have been clipping newspaper stories about South Carolina's various quality-of-life indexes. You know — average income, life expectancy, infant mortality, obesity, violence, drop-out rate — the kind of things you might want to know if you were thinking about moving here or bringing your company here.

I use the numbers to write a column periodically or to update the little civic talk I am occasionally asked to deliver. And the numbers are always troubling. As you probably know, our state generally ranks first in the worst and last in the best. It is a tradition we share with most of the Southern states. In fact, the joke is that only one state keeps us from being dead last in everything — hence, the oft-spoken benediction, "Thank God for Mississippi."

Well, it looks like my newspaper-clipping days are over. The Center for a Better South, based in Charleston, has just released its *2011 Briefing Book on the South*, an online statistical profile of the region (bettersouth.org/publications), using 36 indicators and more than 70 data points from an array of sources for each Southern state.

The Better South report provides a wealth of data about the Palmetto State; for example, South Carolina has the 10th-highest poverty rate in the nation and ranks fifth in child poverty. We have the second-highest rate of food insecurity — it used to be called hunger — and we are the sixth-worst place to raise children.

We rank eighth in diabetes, eighth in obesity, fifth in infant mortality, fourth in premature births, 11th in births to teen mothers, and 12th in adult smoking.

Want some education numbers? We are next to last in the nation in high school graduation rates; 62.2 percent of public high school students graduate on time. Perhaps one reason for this is that we have the 19th lowest level of expenditure per student in our public schools, at $10,051.

And we are a violent state, ranking fifth in violent crime, seventh in domestic violence, and third in traffic fatalities.

Get the picture?

These bad numbers illustrate a nexus of ancient social and political pathologies. Here's one I found of particular interest: Despite what our Republican governor and legislature would have you believe, we have the eighth-lowest tax burden in the nation, at 8.1 percent of personal income. If lower taxes were the key to jobs and prosperity, South Carolina would be booming, instead of carrying the fourth-highest level of unemployment in the country.

All these numbers were made possible by Andy Brack, founder and president of the Center for a Better South. "A hundred and fifty years after shots were fired at Fort Sumter, we have a Civil War hangover," Brack told me last week. "We have not invested in education and infrastructure." (And with the eighth-lowest tax rate in the nation, it is not likely we will start soon.)

Speaking of the South generally, he said, "It's amazing when you look at statistics across the board. We really are at the bottom of the nation. We have made progress, but so has the rest of the country. We still lag. We are still trying to catch up."

In ranking the states with the lowest household income, Southern states hold eight of the bottom 10 positions; South Carolina is number eight. But there is good news in the survey, Brack said. Virginia ranked number 44, showing that a Southern state could break out of the pack and become a leader.

"Southern states can be mainstream," Brack said. "Virginia raises the standard for everyone."

If the *2011 Briefing Book* is to have any impact, someone has to read it. Brack sent it out electronically two weeks ago to 1,500 academics, policymakers, media figures, and legislators around the region.

That's a good start, but beyond reading the report, policymakers and lawmakers have to care. They have to give a damn. And this is where law and policy have failed in the South for centuries. The people who run this state — and all the southern states — are quite comfortable with things as they are. And there is no reason to think this will change soon. The only people who could make those smug, greedy bastards give a damn do not go to the polls on Election Day.

You see, South Carolina has the 11th lowest rate of voter participation in the nation, based on 2008 election figures. And that number will soon be dropping. Our General Assembly just passed a voter ID law that will potentially disenfranchise 180,000 more South Carolinians.

This poor, old state is broken and dysfunctional in so many ways, and most of them can be traced to the ballot box.

October 19, 2011

(A weakened form of this voter ID law took effect in January 2013.)

PREYING AT THE STATEHOUSE
WHY DO WE KEEP VOTING FOR THE SAME OLD HUCKSTERS?

Standing before the cameras at North Charleston City Hall two weeks ago, Sen. Glenn McConnell looked like he was the one pleading guilty to ethics violations and resigning his office. Instead, the grim-faced politician was stepping up from the post of Senate president pro tempore to the office of lieutenant governor.

But, in yet another example of South Carolina's bizarre and byzantine politics, McConnell's move was universally regarded as a demotion for the man who was regarded as the most powerful player in state politics. As *Post and Courier* columnist Brian Hicks quipped, McConnell will get to bang the gavel and wear a purple robe — and little else. It's a big comedown for the man who used to run the state Senate like his own private circus.

McConnell is to be commended for accepting this "demotion," if not quite accepting it with grace. It was assumed by many — including this observer — that he would use his notorious parliamentary skills to sidestep the ceremonial lieutenant governor's office.

Although there was speculation that McConnell would be running for his one-time Senate seat in November, the lieutenant governor announced last week that he would accept his fate. However, all of the drama and confusion over this change-up at the Statehouse probably means we will be voting soon on another amendment to patch our state's woefully inadequate and ill-conceived constitution.

But enough about Glenn McConnell. This constitutional crisis was brought on by Lt. Gov. Ken Ard, who was indicted on criminal ethics charges for campaign fraud and misuse of campaign contributions for personal expenses.

The details of the scheme do not matter. What is important is that yet another Statehouse occupant has preyed on the public trust and has been forced from office. Ard is just the latest in a long and colorful tradition of scandal in the Statehouse and beyond, including Operation Lost Trust, a federal sting resulting in the conviction of more than 20 members of the General Assembly, lobbyists, and other state officials on various bribery and corruption charges; Operation Abscam, another federal sting that led to the conviction of Congressman John Jenrette on bribery and corruption charges; and countless other crimes and misdemeanors leading to the downfall of lesser public figures.

This is not to say that South Carolina is the most corrupt state in the nation — not by a long shot. We cannot measure up to New Jersey, Louisiana, Illinois, and maybe a few others. But what I think makes us distinct is the level of insufferable public piety we provide as a backdrop to our public corruption.

Does any state offer more Bible-thumping, more prayers and preaching in the public forum than South Carolina? (OK, maybe Mississippi.) And has this shameless behavior made us better people? Has it made our leaders wiser or more honest? The levels of violence, ignorance, poverty, disease, and other quality-of-life indexes would suggest not. And yet we continue to preach and pray and whoop and shout and expect our leaders to do the same. But the truth is that religion is the force that divides us, holds us back, and distracts us from real problems and real solutions.

Of course, most of these distractions involve sex. Right now there are several bills in the General Assembly designed to make it more difficult for women to obtain abortions. Paradoxically (or hypocritically), the same Christian elements that do not want women to have access to abortion services have fought for years to keep sex education out of schools, thus assuring that South Carolina will continue to have one of the highest rates of teen pregnancy and sexually transmitted disease in the nation. Another bill would levy a $100 fine on teens for "sexting." Do our legislators really have nothing better to do? There are still no state laws to protect LGBTs from discrimination in the workplace, but, in 2006, the Christian Right whipped up a great moral crusade to amend our poor old state constitution to ban same-sex marriage.

Now it seems that the Almighty wants South Carolina to have a state Day of Prayer and Charleston Rep. Chip Limehouse has obliged him with a bill to that effect. I don't know whether Limehouse is pandering to God or to the voters when he says, "I would hope every day would be a day of prayer ... and to those who object, my [question] is, 'Why would we not have prayer in our lives?'"

And my question to all the panderers and the preachers is: Why can't we just govern with good fact-based policy and compassion, rather than false piety and ideology? We may or may not have less public corruption, but we will surely have more sound and wise government.

March 21, 2012

ETHICALLY CHALLENGED
IT'S TIME TO CRACK DOWN ON CORRUPTION IN COLUMBIA

In 1989, FBI agents moved into the demimonde of bars and clubs around the Statehouse in Columbia and set up a massive sting called Operation Lost Trust. Over the next two years, they offered bribes to legislators to support a sucker bill to legalize horse- and dog-track betting. Too many South Carolina lawmakers were happy to sell their votes.

When the feds sprang the Lost Trust trap in 1991, they snared 17 General Assembly members, seven lobbyists, and three others on bribery, extortion, and drug charges. All but one were convicted or pleaded guilty.

The epic sting and convictions made for riveting reading and reverberated around the nation. It even shocked this jaded old state, which has seen just about everything. In the end, archaic ethics laws were rewritten, and legislators swore they had found religion. It was going to be a new day in Columbia. From now on, there would be clean government, sunshine, transparency, and accountability.

That was a generation ago, and apparently all those pledges and lofty intentions have been forgotten, as demonstrated by recent reports from the Capital City. First, there is Gov. Nikki Haley, who faces a House Ethics Committee investigation. While she was in the House of Representatives, she was on the payroll of a Lexington County hospital at the same time she was pushing legislation the hospital desperately wanted.

In an apparent effort to distract the Ethics Committee and the public, Haley's attorney has promised to make public a list of other legislators who have received money from organizations that lobby at the Statehouse. Whose names are on that list and who are they working for? What legislation have they written or advanced to benefit their paymasters? That's a revelation we can look forward to in the weeks ahead — that is, if Haley's attorneys ever produce the much-talked-about list.

In the meantime, Haley and her attorney have cited attorney-client privilege in declining to surrender e-mails sought by the Ethics Committee in their investigation. Haley is beginning to sound like Richard Nixon.

Last week, in a stunning revelation, *The Post and Courier* reported that in recent years Rep. Jim Merrill, the powerful Daniel Island Republican, has been on the payroll of the S.C. Association of Realtors. While receiving some $158,000 in consulting fees from the Realtors, he was the "primary sponsor and leading voice on legislation" to cut property taxes, making it easier for Realtors to sell houses.

Not only did his one-man consulting firm handle direct mail for the Realtors, but "Merrill's work included advising the Realtors as to which legislators would fall in line with their priorities so the group could back those lawmakers' campaigns," the *P&C* reported. The Charleston daily also notes that the group paid Merrill to design an ad that appeared in newspapers around the state, urging further tax cuts by the state House of Representatives.

Was there anything wrong in what Merrill, Haley, and perhaps others in the General Assembly are doing when they take money from special interests who lobby the Assembly? Sadly, the answer is no, according to the staff of the House Ethics Committee. "There's nothing unethical about it whatsoever," Merrill declared, citing the staff of the Ethics Committee as his legal authority.

And Merrill had something else to say, something that was even more troubling: "The General Assembly doesn't mean that much to me. I'm to the point that I have been there long enough to be jaded now, so my I-don't-give-a-damn meter is way off the charts."

A couple of observations about this sterling public servant and his colleagues in Columbia: First, Merrill will be re-elected in November because he has no opposition, nor has he had any since 2002. "I guess they think I'm doing a pretty good job," he said of his constituents. I guess they do.

My second point is that a number of people outside the Statehouse think that what is going on there stinks. Armand Derfner, a prominent public interest lawyer, told the *P&C* that Merrill's behavior in other states would be deemed "unethical and criminal, but here in South Carolina, it's the norm."

Edwin Bender, executive director of the National Institute on Money in State Politics, said of Columbia, "That's the political culture and that is a very hard thing to change." Indeed, he suggested it might be time for another federal intervention in Columbia to clean house and drain the cesspool. He didn't say it, but I will: We need another Operation Lost Trust.

All of these revelations come less than four months after Lt. Gov. Ken Ard pleaded guilty to campaign law violations and resigned his office. And thanks in part to these unfortunate events, South Carolina feels evermore like a Third World country — Afghanistan, perhaps, or Haiti — where Uncle Sam tries to impose democracy and modern values only to have its efforts thwarted every time by tribal leaders and special interests. You can't save those who don't wish to be saved.

June 20, 2012

(Neither Haley nor her attorney ever released the promised list of legislators who worked for companies with lobbyists. Jim Merrill still represents Daniel Island in Columbia. State Sen. Robert Ford, of Chaleston, resigned his seat in 2013 and awaits trial on numerous ethics and criminal charges. And House Speaker Bobby Harrell resigned his seat and agreed to cooperate with prosecutors after pleading guilty to multiple ethics violations in October 2014.)

TOLERANCE IS GOOD BUSINESS
OUR GAY INDEX IS ABOUT ECONOMIC DEVELOPMENT AS MUCH AS SEXUAL PREFERENCE

For a state that loves the free market as much as South Carolina claims to, we hand out a hell of a lot of corporate welfare for companies to come here and do business. And to hear the politicians and boosters tell it, it's all done with the best intentions. After all, these new businesses are creating jobs and expanding the tax base. But anyone who understands the politics and the culture of this state must be suspicious that at least part of their motivation is the warm feeling they get from giving money to rich people.

In recent decades, this state and its counties and municipalities have doled out hundreds of millions of dollars in economic development incentives to companies like BMW, Boeing, Michelin, and many others, mostly in the form of tax breaks, but also special infrastructure improvements, employee training, and other plums. Nothing is too good for a company that will promise to come here and build a plant.

Has it worked? Well, that depends on what you mean by "work." I'm sure a few people would say that giving companies millions of dollars for doing what they intend to do anyway is just swell. And there is no question that developers and financial service providers have made a lot of money here in recent years. But our roads and schools are more crowded than ever, our infrastructure is crumbling, and our air and water are threatened. South Carolina schools still rank among the worst in the nation. We still have among the lowest standards of living and personal income. We still have among the shortest life expectancies and highest infant mortality rates. Go down the list of quality-of-life indexes and South Carolina remains among the worst places to live, based on all quantifiable data.

What do entrepreneurs and corporate executives look for when they go shopping for a site for a new factory or corporate headquarters? Richard Florida set out to answer this question in his 2002 book, *The Rise of the Creative Class*. As Florida explained to Minnesota Public Radio, he wanted to know if the key to economic development was not where companies decide to locate, but where people choose to live. He compared a list of powerhouse high-tech cities assembled by one research institute with the gay index — a list of cities with disproportionately large gay populations — compiled by another researcher looking at similar questions. "And lo and behold, the lists looked the same," Florida said.

Smart companies are looking for smart people, not just a public dole. These are the people Florida calls the Creative Class. They are scientists, engineers, architects, designers, writers, artists, musicians, and anyone else who uses creativity as a key factor in their business or profession. The Creative Class comprises some 40 million members and more than 30 percent of the nation's workforce. It will continue to shape our economy and culture for generations.

If South Carolina was smart, we would not be cutting taxes to the bone, as Gov. Nikki Haley and her GOP allies in Columbia advocate. We would not be throwing money at companies and begging them to come here. We would be building our infrastructure, improving our schools, developing our cultural amenities, and producing an atmosphere that creative people would want to live in.

One way to do that is to put out the welcome mat, to announce to the world that South Carolina is a diverse and tolerant place, that we do not discriminate on the basis of race or creed, gender, or sexual orientation. In other words, it might be time for us to improve our gay index. So here is my suggestion for developing our economy and making our state a more free and livable place: This Saturday at 11 a.m., the third annual Charleston Pride Festival parade will strike out from Park Circle in North Charleston and head down Montague Avenue to Virginia Avenue. It's a short route, so it should be easy to schedule and easy to participate, either as a walker or an observer. Anyone who is serious about making South Carolina a magnet for industry and business should be there. That goes for Nikki Haley and every official who supported subsidies to bring Boeing to town.

Such a gesture would send a very clear message that South Carolina is open for business and that we are a tolerant and welcoming society, looking for smart, creative people to bring their brains and talent here. Business and industry will follow.

That's a bold strategy for this conservative old state, and it would cost taxpayers nothing. If our leaders were really leaders, they would join in Saturday's rally. We will see who shows up.

July 11, 2012

SECRECY AND CYNICISM
SOUTH CAROLINA'S GOVERNMENT IS BUILT ON THEM

The worst-governed state in America — that's the way I have described South Carolina many times over the past 10 years, and I have previously shown the numbers to prove it. There's no need to repeat them here other than to say that in almost every national quality-of-life index — be it income, education level, life expectancy, infant mortality, violent crime, or environmental quality — we place near the bottom.

Part of South Carolina's problem is the historic resistance of our leaders — and much of its white population — to the laws and culture of the United States. We saw it in the nullification crisis of 1832, the days leading up to secession and the Civil War, and the resistance to all civil rights and voting rights legislation in the past century. All of these federal laws have had the purpose of improving democracy and creating a higher quality of life in this backward, benighted little state. Most recently our state was at the U.S. Supreme Court fighting the Affordable Care Act. Gov. Nikki Haley and the GOP legislature are sworn to resist the ACA's insurance exchanges, which are intended to provide healthcare to the poor.

This angry, obstructionist behavior by white state leaders is part of a pattern of anti-democratic governance that has held South Carolina back. We saw two other examples of this behavior in the news recently.

The first was a report by the Voting Integrity Program at Common Cause, which declared that South Carolina was among six states that were unprepared to deal with voting machine failures on Election Day. According to the report, we are one of 16 states that still use paperless voting machines.

"If those machines malfunction, there's no way to independently check what the actual voter's intent was," said a spokeswoman for the Voting Integrity Project. "In these 16 states, we're very vulnerable to miscounts that won't be caught."

But if you have been following the news in recent months, you know that this is not the voting problem the General Assembly seeks to address. Following the national Republican playbook, our legislature has passed a voter ID law to prevent voter fraud, yet there has been no evidence of voter impersonation in this state in decades. What this law will likely do, according to the League of Women Voters and the ACLU, is disenfranchise nearly 200,000 poor and elderly voters. The U.S. Justice Department has challenged the law in federal court.

That our General Assembly would ignore real and proven voting machine problems, while going to extreme and expensive measures to fix a nonexistent voting problem and in the process disenfranchise much of the electorate, says all that needs to be said about our leaders' agenda.

And yet, there is more to say. The day after the Voting Integrity Program released its report, another independent agency, the State Integrity Investigation, ranked the Palmetto State as the worst in the country for access to public records.

The Post and Courier reported that the state earned a big fat F for transparency. The State Integrity Investigation cited a lack of options for citizens – outside of court action – in appealing a denied public information request. And the state has no agency to monitor the application of its freedom of information law.

Jay Bender, an attorney for the S.C. Press Association, said the root of our state's transparency problem is a deep and ancient culture of secrecy, dating back to colonial times, when a "thin band of elites" ran the government.

"We took that cultural model directly from the plantation to the mill village, and in many ways that remains the dominant political culture in South Carolina," Bender told the *P&C*.

Anyone who has practiced journalism in this state for a while knows how difficult it is to get information from public agencies that do not want to surrender it. Not only does it make for bad governance, but it makes for bad journalism. After all, a secretive public culture makes it difficult for journalists to do their job. And without good journalism, good government is impossible.

So we have here a perfect storm of bad government. Not only do the citizens of South Carolina have little power to learn what their leaders are doing, but if they were to find out, there is little they could do about it. Voter suppression, coupled with unreliable voting technology, undermines the legitimacy of elections and of elected officials. The result is a cynical public and the worst-governed state in America.

August 8, 2012

FEAR & THE GOP

"This is the future of this [Republican] Party, right here in the South."

— *Richard Nixon,*
Columbia, S.C., 1966

SO LONG, CARROLL
SAY HELLO TO STROM FOR US

The death last week of former Gov. Carroll Campbell offers an opportunity to look back over several decades of sound and fury and to marvel at how little has actually changed in South Carolina politics.

Campbell did for the state political scene what Ronald Reagan did for the national scene -- created a major realignment between the two parties. Campbell was not as disastrous for South Carolina as Reagan is proving to be for the nation, only because this state was already a social and economic wreck when he was elected governor in 1986.

Not everyone shares my sardonic opinion of the late governor. Under the headline, "Carroll Campbell's stellar legacy," the editorial writers at *The Post and Courier* predictably described Campbell as "a state hero, role model, visionary, and inspiration." The *P&C* eulogists mentioned state government reorganization, ethics reform of the General Assembly, and luring BMW to Spartanburg County as the major accomplishments of Campbell's administration. True enough. But in the final analysis, South Carolina's standing among the states was not changed by Campbell's exertions. Last in the best, first in the worst. That has been South Carolina's traditional ranking and it was a tradition Campbell left unchallenged.

Campbell's most lasting accomplishment, of course, was to solidify the Republican hold on political power in the state. When he became governor, the Democrats controlled both houses of the General Assembly, and the white population was evenly divided in its loyalty between Republicans and Democrats. When he left office eight years later, Republicans controlled the Assembly and most whites identified themselves as Republican. Campbell accomplished this by subtle manipulation of words and symbols -- including the Confederate flag -- to let whites know that the Republican Party was now their party.

Carroll Campbell could herd white people the way a border collie herds sheep. A bark here, a bite there; he could keep them agitated and running until he got them where he wanted them. Today, most of the white people in South Carolina are in the Republican Party fold, grazing and bleating contentedly. And why not? With the Confederate flag flying in front of the Statehouse and gays firmly under control, what more could a citizen ask for?

But there is an even darker side of the Campbell legacy, one that is almost completely forgotten. Today, the politics of fear and division, smear and innuendo are more deeply ingrained in our national politics than ever before. And it was two men, more than any others, who brought us to this shameful impasse. One was South Carolina native and political operative Lee Atwater; the other was his friend and colleague Karl Rove, who created George W. Bush from a lump of ignorance.

In 1978, Carroll Campbell was running for Congress in the fourth district. His Democratic opponent was Greenville Mayor Max Heller. Atwater was working for the Campbell campaign and the race was close. Campbell's pollsters had asked several questions regarding religion and ethnicity, and learned that voters could overlook Heller's being a Jewish immigrant, but they could not vote for a man who did not accept Jesus Christ as his savior.

Enter one Don Sprouse, a third-party candidate and high school dropout who had never run for political office before and never would again. Two days before the election, Sprouse held a news conference to remind the good people of the fourth district that Heller was, indeed, a Jew who did not "believe that Jesus has come yet." He went on to say that a Jew should not represent South Carolina's fourth congressional district.

Campbell won that election and was on his way to Congress and later the governor's office. He denied knowing anything about Don Sprouse or setting him up to play the religion card against Heller. Perhaps he was telling the truth, but Atwater was happy to take credit for the deed.

Atwater would go on to manage the George H.W. Bush presidential campaign in 1988, the campaign in which he masterminded the infamous Willie Horton ad, terrifying white Americans with the image of the black rapist. In the 2000 GOP presidential primary campaign, Karl Rove & Co. won the critical South Carolina primary for GWB with a smear campaign accusing Sen. John McCain of fathering a black child.

Carroll Campbell's life and career came at a critical nexus in American politics. South Carolina was a laboratory for the kind of campaigning that has come to dominate national elections. It worked brilliantly here and operatives like Atwater and Rove learned to apply the techniques to other campaigns and candidates around the country. And while Campbell may or may not have been directly involved, he profited from the practice.

The *P&C*'s hymns notwithstanding, Carroll Campbell was a mean little politician who knew how to win elections in the meanest little state in the nation.

December 14, 2005

WHITE PEOPLE'S PARTY STRIKES AGAIN
REPUBLICANS TRY TO TURN BACK THE CLOCK ON REFORM

In retrospect, the period from about 1970 to 1986 was a sort of Golden Age for South Carolina. African Americans had begun to enter the Democratic Party and get elected to the General Assembly. A group of young progressives were also elected to the Assembly — the Young Turks, they were called — and started shaking things up as they had not been shaken since Reconstruction. Out of that period came a great deal of progressive and long overdue legislation. Among the many laws that were passed were the Home Rule Act, of 1976, and the Education Improvement Act, of 1984, the crowning achievement of the era and of the administration of Gov. Dick Riley.

Two years later, Carroll Campbell was elected governor and set about building a new Republican Party, a majority party, a white party. As the former leader of a march against school busing, he had the credentials to do it. White people abandoned the Democratic Party in droves and white Democratic officeholders switched parties, as Strom Thurmond had done. By 1995, when Campbell left office, the GOP controlled the General Assembly and the Golden Age was over. A dark age of meanness and intolerance had set in, and we can see more evidence of it every day.

Before passage of the Home Rule Act, the counties of South Carolina had no governing councils or administrators. They were run by the counties' legislative delegations. Home Rule decentralized much of the state's power, allowing local jurisdictions to govern themselves. It was one of the most democratic laws ever passed in a state that has little appreciation for democracy.

And it was too good to last. In recent years we have seen the Republican legislature undermining Home Rule, and much of their behavior seems to have a racist tinge to it.

When city leaders in Columbia sought to sue gun manufacturers in an effort to make their streets safer, the General Assembly passed legislation barring such action. Ostensibly, it was done in the name of protecting the Second Amendment right to bear arms. But anyone who understands South Carolina knows that this was more than a constitutional issue. Our solons never let a little thing like the Constitution stand in the way of a sanctimonious law. No, this was an attempt by suburban and rural (i.e., white) legislators to stick it to an urban (i.e., black) region of the state.

Since the Supreme Court struck down the doctrine of separate-but-equal in 1954, certain elements of the white community have fought a guerilla war to undermine public education and re-segregate the schools. One of the tools they have used is school vouchers. Another is charter schools. Some school boards have balked at creating new charter schools, specifically because they tend to become segregated and draw funding away from traditional schools. To address this matter, the General Assembly created a single statewide charter school district, effectively overriding every school board in the state.

Or take the case of Charleston County School Board, which

recently voted to hire a lobbyist to go to Columbia and get them some additional funding. Some lawmakers and community members were infuriated.

"The school board's actions are outrageous," said Rep. John Graham Altman III (R-West Ashley), the most outspoken bigot in the General Assembly. "They are spending taxpayers' money to get more taxpayers' money."

Well, yes, but they are hardly alone. Several of the largest counties and cities in the state — including Charleston — have lobbyists in Columbia. Altman never seemed outraged over that.

Immediately after news of the school lobbyist broke, Rep. Jim Merrill, R-Daniel Island, proposed a bill that would bar the Charleston County School Board from hiring a contract lobbyist. So much for Home Rule. And one can only wonder if this bill is not intended as a slap at the county school superintendent and the lobbyist, both of whom are black.

And consider what happened in Berkeley County recently. When residents didn't like the hike in property taxes to support school construction and renovation, Sen. Larry Grooms, R-Bonneau, swung into action, introducing legislation that would take budgetary power out of the hands of the school board and give it to Berkeley County Council.

"The proposals by Senator Grooms would severely cripple the board's ability to run the district," said Scott Price, general counsel to the S.C. School Boards Association. "All the proposals fly in the face of local control..."

Even Berkeley County Supervisor Jim Rozier thinks it's a bad idea. "My problem is, I can't look at a budget once a year and tell you anything about it," he said.

This is one more example of Republicans out of control. The White People's Party has a stranglehold on state government and they are using it to violate Home Rule and push their right-wing agenda.

February 1, 2006

THE PRESIDENTIAL PRIMARY
SOUTH CAROLINA MAY LOSE ITS ROLE AS KING MAKER

Since 1980, South Carolina has held an exalted place as the "Gateway to Dixie" in that quadrennial marathon that begins with the Iowa caucuses and ends at the White House.

In that year, South Carolina native son and GOP strategist Lee Atwater persuaded the state Republican Party executive committee to pull South Carolina out of the nine-state Big South primary and hold the state GOP primary on the Saturday before the Big South. The thinking was that South Carolina would be the bellwether for Dixie and show other white Southerners how to vote.

That year, Reagan won by a landslide in South Carolina, swept through the Big South primaries three days later and was on his way to the White House. The Palmetto State has held the second GOP primary in the nation ever since, and no Republican has won his party's presidential nomination without first winning in South Carolina.

This has given our state a special relationship with the presidency. Ronald Reagan, George Bush I, and George Bush II have all felt beholden to the state and have shown their appreciation by making numerous trips here during their White House tenure. The state GOP has used the attention as a party-building tool, turning this into one of the most staunchly Republican states in the nation.

Each four years this little state, with its historic inferiority complex and its memories of lost grandeur, becomes the center of the universe, as Republican candidates swarm in like locusts and the national media follow. For white South Carolinians, it's been the greatest surge of testosterone since that memorable morning in 1861 when those shots were fired on Fort Sumter.

Now all that glory may soon be over. The Republican Party of Michigan announced last week that it wants to schedule its presidential primary to take place on the same day as South Carolina's. We would have to share the political visits and the media spotlight with a much larger state.

This should give every South Carolinian — indeed, every American — occasion to ponder the awesome power that has been placed in the hands of the white population of this little state.

Anyone who has read John Brody's *Bad Boy – The Life and Politics of Lee Atwater* knows that Atwater was a restless and tortured soul, who epitomized this restless and tortured state. And his bare-knuckled, hit-and-run, smear-and-innuendo style of politics could be said to epitomize the politics of this state.

More than creating the early primary in South Carolina, Atwater's most important political tactic was bringing Christian evangelicals and fundamentalists, with their sexually obsessed "family values," into the fold of mainstream Republican politics. It took a diabolical genius to make allies of the likes of Bob Jones III and Rupert Murdoch, but the strange alliance has held for a quarter century and has transformed America's politics, government, and national priorities.

And it gave us George W. Bush.

Think back to that February in 2000. In a stunning upset, Sen. John McCain defeated the Texas governor in the New Hampshire primary. One more defeat and Bush's presidential campaign would be over.

Within 12 hours after the votes were tallied in New Hampshire, Bush was on the campus of Bob Jones University in Greenville, reminding right-wing Christians that he was one of them, a born-again, ready to take on abortion and gay rights, ready to fight for prayer in public schools.

Before white Republican voters went to the polls the next Tuesday, they started receiving mysterious phone calls: Were they aware that Sen. McCain's wife was a drug addict? Were they aware that the senator was mentally unstable as a result of his seven-year incarceration as a POW in North Vietnam? Were they aware that the senator had an illegitimate black daughter? All the insinuations were false (and the last one bitterly ironic, in light of later revelations about the late Strom Thurmond), but they derailed McCain's candidacy in South Carolina and sent Bush to the White House.

Now we have a president who wallows with the Christian fundies, who does not believe in evolution or global warming, who opposes stem cell research, who makes war promiscuously, who wiretaps illegally, and who turns our natural resources over to the corporate robber barons. And to look at the bumper stickers around here, the white people of South Carolina would surely do it over again, if given the chance.

George W. Bush is their gift to America.

It was a cruel trick of fate that transformed the most politically and socially dysfunctional state in America into the national king maker.

Michigan's decision to challenge our presidential primary with their own means that South Carolina will lose its moment in the spotlight. Thank God! Every time this state gets a little attention, it makes a fool of itself.

April 5, 2006

(The South Carolina GOP primary remains the first in the South and the second in the nation.)

EMINENT DOMAIN
RADICAL REPUBLICANS THREATEN PROPERTY VALUES

In a state that was founded on the principle of human slavery, it is not surprising that some people still hold property rights to be the highest value in society.

This principle is being tested in the General Assembly right now as the state Senate debates what to do with House Bill 4503, the most recent attempt by Republican extremists to enact property rights protections so radical as to essentially end all zoning and land use planning in South Carolina.

Under H. 4503, county and municipal governments would be required to pay landowners if public zoning decisions prevented landowners from obtaining the full speculative value of their property. Purported to be a law that protects property values, it would in fact have the opposite effect, according to William L. Want, professor of land use law at the Charleston School of Law.

Writing recently in *The Post and Courier*, Want stated, "If a coastal community zoned to prevent 10-story hotels or other communities zoned to prevent industrial facilities or hog farms next to homes, they would have to pay off the developers using our tax dollars." The cost would be prohibitive, essentially ending all efforts by communities to maintain quality of life by environmental or aesthetic zoning.

"Behemoth beachfront hotels and pig farms are lining up at the state's borders," Want warns.

In working this bill through the House, Republicans have once again played the plutocrat-in-populist-clothing gig. Whenever they seek to screw the little guy in the name of the corporations, they first dress up like the little guy to lead him into the trap. In this case, they put on overalls and the rhetorical straw hat, pretending they were out to protect Old McDonald and rest of the farmers and small land-owners from those urban politicians and bureaucrats who wanted to control their land.

Don't be fooled.

The man who introduced H. 4503 was none other than Rep. Tracy Edge (R-North Myrtle Beach). When he is not in Columbia leading the crusade against sane land use policy, Edge works as vice president of the Burroughs & Chapin Co., the giant developer that created Myrtle Beach and keeps it under the corporate thumb. (For the inside story on how B&C controls its Horry County fiefdom, see my online book, *Banana Republic Revisited – 75 Years of Madness, Mayhem & Minigolf in Myrtle Beach*.)

Burroughs & Chapin's assault on the democratic process — both in Horry County and in Richland County, where it has been angling for years to create a giant development on the Congaree River flood plain — is so egregious that it is no wonder that the corporate giant would dispatch its lieutenant to lead the legislative assault on local sovereignty.

"Local government is the core component of our democracy and much of what it deals with involves land use," writes Want. "The S.C. House bill would take away this local authority and place land use decisions in the hands of any individual who cares to operate completely at odds with the will of the community."

The reason the radical property rights crowd — led by the real estate lobby — think this is the year they might actually succeed in passing their "regulatory takings" legislation is because they have piggy-backed it onto another bill that is almost sure to pass. In 2005, the U.S. Supreme Court ruled that the City of New Bedford, Conn., could seize private property for use by other private interests, if it were done for the "greater public good" of economic development.

State lawmakers went into a tizzy to make sure nothing like that ever happens in South Carolina. Sen. Chip Campsen (R-Charleston) proposed a constitutional amendment to prevent eminent domain from ever being used in such a manner as it was in Connecticut. It was probably unnecessary. The state Supreme Court has consistently held that eminent domain could be used only to take land for public use. But the amendment passed the Senate, and radical property rights advocates in the House saw this as the vehicle to move their agenda forward. H. 4503 is an amendment to Campsen's constitutional amendment.

There is evidence that cooler heads will prevail in Columbia. The *P&C* has editorialized against H. 4503 twice in recent weeks. The Coastal Conservation League is rallying opposition to H. 4503. In one recent e-message to their supporters, the CCL wrote that "Rather than being a boon to landowners, the takings bill would be an 'Attorney and Appraisers Relief Act.'"

In his syndicated column, *Statehouse Report*, Andy Brack also took on H. 4503, saying, "the House bill would put private interests ahead of community interests." Brack quoted Want as saying. "Let's hope lawmakers exercise better judgment throughout the rest of the session, particularly when it comes to land use."

Let's hope.

April 19, 2006

(H.4503 ultimately passed the House, but did not make it out of the Senate.)

THE PEOPLE HAVE SPOKEN
AND WHAT VACUOUS PRATTLE IT WAS

"Whichever party best combines noble causes and monsters and clinches its claim to the banner of God will win. Party labels may or may not be changed. In any case, I believe, the mind of the South will remain the same."

—*W.J. Cash*

The people of South Carolina went to the polls last week to finish the business of nominating candidates for office in November's general election. Whatever else came out of this exercise in democracy, it demonstrates that the Republican Party is as intellectually and morally bankrupt as Enron.

Indeed, party labels have changed since Cash wrote those words for *the American Mercury* in 1929. The morally and intellectually bankrupt Democratic Party of 80 years ago is the Republican Party of 2006. The event that triggered this switch in party labels was the civil rights movement and its resulting legislation, which was shepherded through Congress by the national Democratic Party. White Southerners retaliated by switching party allegiance from Democratic to Republican.

The great party label switch is now essentially complete. Sixty years ago, Democrats controlled every seat in the General Assembly, all statewide constitutional offices; both U.S. senators and all six U.S. representatives were Democrats. South Carolina was a backward little banana republic of corruption and political infighting, where black people were barred from holding political office.

In 1994, the Republicans took control of both houses of the General Assembly for the first time since Reconstruction. With the November elections, it's a safe bet that the GOP will control all nine statewide offices, both U.S. Senate seats and four of six U.S. House seats. Today, South Carolina is a backward little banana republic of corruption and political infighting, where black people are effectively barred from political power.

In the recent primary campaigns, the Republican candidates repeated their relentless mantra of tax cuts and school vouchers.
In a recent to trip to Horry County, I saw a sign for a local Republican candidate: "He Protects Our Pocket."

In all the political advertising I observed over the past few weeks, I did not see a single Republican boasting that he protects our environment, protects our civil rights, protects our schools. Those things cost money, of course, and apparently the white people of South Carolina care more about their money than they do about the commonwealth of our state. The result of this old and unchallenged behavior is that South Carolina perennially ranks near the bottom of the nation for such quality-of-life indexes as education, personal income, life expectancy, crime, infant mortality, highway deaths — and the list goes on.

The utter predictability with which white people vote Republican can only be compared to some totemic ritual. As the Democratic Party was for generations of their ancestors, the modern Republican Party has become a near mystical bond of kinship for white voters and, in the South, kinship and mystical bonds trump common sense and sound public policy.

As a demonstration of how strong these white tribal bonds are, Lt. Governor André Bauer placed thousands of roadside signs around the state with the simple message: "André -- Republican."

Since he apparently stands for nothing (except lowering taxes, of course) and his political resumé could be written on a matchbook, he really had little to recommend himself except that he is white — in other words, Republican.

Perhaps no recent election better demonstrates white tribal instincts better than Bauer's first election as lieutenant governor four years ago. White voters elected him over Democratic rival Phil Leventis, a leader on environmental and education issues in the state Senate and perhaps the closest thing to a statesman we have in the General Assembly today. He was also a decorated veteran of Gulf War I and a brigadier general in the Air National Guard.

Since becoming lieutenant governor, Bauer has regularly embarrassed himself and the state with his very public traffic offenses and knack for reaping a windfall from the sale of property to the state. Now he is about to be rewarded with a second term.

In a recent editorial, the Myrtle Beach *Sun News* opined: "Decades of backbiting, infighting, and arrogant behavior caught up with the Democrats in time, and they lost their power here and nationally ... The same will happen to the Republicans unless they figure out how to govern with a semblance of unity and humility."

I disagree. Republicans don't have to be unified or humble. They are white and whites are in the majority. And that's how democracy works in South Carolina.

July 5, 2006

LIVING IN FEAR
IN THIS STATE, FEAR IS A LIFESTYLE CHOICE FOR MOST VOTERS

I have written for years that the great force holding South Carolina back from social and economic development is fear — fear of black people, fear of secularism, fear of sex, fear of the future itself. Events in recent weeks offer ample support for my contention.

Demagogues dominated the political landscape in this state for generations, herding white people around like so many sheep, keeping society divided against itself and distracted from the real challenges the state faced. Their tactics were colorful and inflammatory and their bogeyman was always the threat of "race mixing." The age of the fire-breathing, race-baiting demagogue is gone. He has been replaced by the pinstriped "public interest advocate."

The most mendacious example of this today is South Carolinians for Responsible Government, a "grassroots" organization, which has either 2,000 or 200,000 members, depending on whom they are talking to, and who are funded by one Howard Rich, a millionaire Libertarian who writes huge checks to South Carolina Republicans from his New York City apartment. It is SCRG that is pushing Gov. Mark Sanford's "Put Parents in Charge" voucher plan and so far Rich has given $30,000 to Sanford and $40,000 to Karen Floyd, the GOP candidate for superintendent of education. In so doing, he's flouted the intent of the state's $3,500 campaign contribution limits and has sued the State Ethics Commission for trying to hold him to those limits. (The executive director of SCRG recently resigned after he was caught sending letters to the editor of *The State* newspaper under false names. More "grassroots" organizing, no doubt.)

In the Republican primaries last June, SCRG funded several right-wing candidates who knocked off moderate Republicans who had failed to support Sanford's voucher plan. Of course, the voucher scheme is little more than a "respectable" way to re-segregate South Carolina's schools and suck the lifeblood out of public education in this state.

Now South Carolinians for Responsible Government has cast its lot in two local House district races. Two weeks ago, I wrote about the glossy, four-color flyer which SCRG mailed out to thousands of Republican voters in District 115, attacking Democrat Eugene Platt, not on any issues or political positions, but on his poetry. Yes, his poetry!

In screaming headlines, the SCRG denounced Platt's character and accused him of "deviant sexual behavior" for penning lines such as this:

"Our weekly passion spent, we fall apart on sheets
Illicitly stained before us by legions of lovers like us,
and savor mirrored forms lying side by side overhead.
Beside the bed a digital clock signals, then,
the end of another hour of stolen bliss..."

Speaking last week on a local radio call-in program, Platt said, "I would challenge my opponent, here in the presence of God and, by extension, your listening audience, to condemn this mailing as one of the most dastardly acts in the history of South Carolina politics."

His opponent, incumbent Republican Wallace Scarborough, has not condemned the SCRG flyer. He understands the power of sexual innuendo among the sexually repressed white folk of District 115.

Then, last week, SCRG sent a flyer to Republican voters in District 119, charging Democratic candidate Leon Stavrinakis, as a member of Charleston County Council, with supporting a pro-drug special interest group. What the flyer referred to was the council grant of $500 to South Carolinians for Drug Law Reform, a registered 501(c)(4) lobbying group based in Charleston. Not only did Stavrinakis oppose the grant (which was made by another council member), but the $500 was later returned because SCDLR did not meet all council stipulations for the grant. But none of that was explained in the flyer. It was just another smear job by SCRG, trying to play on people's irrational fears.

Politicians have so successfully linked the fear of crime to the fear of drugs that it is impossible to separate the two in any public discourse. Any politician who suggests that legalizing drugs would go far toward reducing the violence on our streets would meet the same fate as Stavrinakis, who had the misfortune of just being in the room where another council member made a grant to South Carolinians for Drug Law Reform.

So it seems that our fear has doomed us to fight this "war on drugs" until hell freezes over, while gangs and thugs fight it out on the streets over turf and nickel bags. Two weeks ago Mayor Joe Riley went to Columbia to present the General Assembly with his crime-fighting wish list. There was no mention of drug education or rehabilitation; just longer sentences, more laws, more cops, more courts, more prisons.

In South Carolina, we cannot afford a decent education system, safe roads, environmental protection, or Medicaid. But there is always money to protect us from our most irrational fears.

October 18, 2006

POSTMORTEM ON ELECTION '06
EVIDENCE POINTS TO SUPERSTITION, MONEY, AND RACISM

Last week's midterm elections were a triumph for moderation and common sense. Democrats made major congressional gains and won governorships in all regions of the country – except the South, of course, where centuries of ignorance, superstition, and fear allow the Republican Party to keep its death grip.

The best evidence of this could be seen in South Carolina's statewide races, where the Republicans swept eight of the nine offices on the ballot. At this writing, Democrat Jim Rex held a lead of fewer than 400 votes for state superintendent of education. What all this means, of course, is that the majority of white South Carolinians still walk in lockstep with the GOP, just as their parents and grandparents walked in lockstep with the Democratic Party in their effort to retain white political control in South Carolina.

As long as a majority of whites continue to give their votes uncritically to Republicans, South Carolina will remain a one-party state and a Third World country. A generation from now, Republican candidates will still be touting their conservative credentials while calling for change and reform. What is clear in this muddled message is that change and reform are needed, but white South Carolinians are in love with the past. We will remain trapped in the past — economically and socially — as long as whites are locked in their racial attitudes, as long as blacks are locked out of political power by the white majority.

But maybe the glass was half-full on Election Day. The good news is that most of the statewide races were relatively close, with Republicans receiving less than 55 percent of the vote. The trend in recent years has been toward closer statewide races, suggesting that racial attitudes are softening, that the influx of new residents is changing this state's culture of fear and intolerance. It gives us hope that someday South Carolina may actually be a two-party state and race will cease to be the dividing line on every issue.

Of course, the issue that brings out the strongest racial animosities is education. For years, South Carolina whites have sought to resegregate education through private schools. And the way they seek to do this is with vouchers, giving public money to families to take their children out of public schools.

Gov. Mark Sanford has his own version of a voucher plan. It is a tax rebate to be used for private education. It is a terrible plan. The money in question is not enough to pay for a private school education. It is just another giveaway to wealthy families who don't need the money and who intend to send their children to private schools anyway.

The Sanford voucher plan was supported by Karen Floyd, the Republican candidate for superintendent of education. More importantly, it was supported by Howard Rich of New York and his many allies and associates, who poured tens of thousands of dollars into Sanford's and Floyd's campaigns. The apparent defeat of Floyd represents a triumph of local interests over out-of-state interests and — hopefully — the end of Sanford's voucher plan.

The bad news comes in the form of the constitutional amendments. The passage of Question 4, capping property assessment at 15 percent every five years, represents a further shift of the tax burden from the wealthiest South Carolinians to middle- and working-class families. Many of the 68 percent of the voters who supported this constitutional amendment are obviously the same people who shop at Walmart and have no health insurance, but vote Republican. This amendment represents a deepening of our class divisions and our state's standing in the Third World.

And, of course, there was Question 1 — the "gay marriage" amendment. This amendment, which formally defined marriage as a union between a man and a woman, was approved by more than 75 percent of voters, demonstrating how deeply imbued this state remains in homophobic superstition. It also demonstrates how quickly black people forget.

Forty years ago, it was blacks who were fighting for basic rights — the right to public accommodations, the right to a decent education, and the right for two people to marry, even if they were of different races, even if Southern laws forbade it and Southern churches called it unnatural and ungodly. The overwhelming majority by which the amendment passed means that not only a majority of whites but also a majority of blacks oppose gay marriage.

Middle-class blacks tend to be very culturally conservative. That's no secret. But it would be nice if they tempered their conservatism with a little respect for other minorities who seek justice and fairness.

In short, little has changed in South Carolina with the recent elections and that, in a nutshell, is the history of this state.

November 15, 2006

STATEHOUSE COUP
REPUBLICANS SHOW THE ARROGANCE OF POWER

Last November, the voters showed their disgust with Congress by throwing out the Republicans and ending their 12-year reign of arrogance and corruption.

House Majority Leader Tom DeLay spoke often of a "permanent Republican majority" in the Congress and apparently believed it. His "K Street Project" -- an insidious alliance of congressional Republicans and Washington lobbyists -- was designed to cement that "permanent majority" through lobbyists' money and DeLay's ruthless tactics.

Those tactics included holding the vote open for three hours on a critical 2003 Medicare reform bill while GOP floor managers twisted enough arms to get the bill passed, and changing House Ethics Committee rules to protect DeLay when he came under criminal investigation.

In the November elections, voters observed these abuses of congressional power (to say nothing of the line of Republicans and lobbyists doing the "perp walk" through federal court) and decided enough is enough. That's the way a healthy democracy works.

Something interesting happened at the Statehouse in Columbia last week and it bears chilling similarity to recent GOP behavior in Washington.

For years Republican leaders have been pushing to have their General Assembly caucus meetings closed to the public, in violation of the state Freedom of Information Act. Last May, state Attorney General Henry McMaster issued an opinion that said, in effect, that the Republican Caucus is not above the law. They are public officials meeting in a public building on public business. They are bound by the FOIA, like any county council or school board or public service commission.

As McMaster wrote in that opinion, a legislative caucus is a "de facto policy-making body ... A citizen does not intelligently participate in the legislative decision-making process merely by witnessing the final tallying of an already predetermined vote."

On the day that Governor Mark Sanford used his State of the State Address to warn the General Assembly about the abuse of power, a majority of House Republicans -- led by a Lowcountry cabal -- pulled a coup that essentially sets the GOP Caucus above the law and the opinion of the Attorney General.

While the media were gathered on the second floor of the Statehouse in anticipation of the governor's address, the House Rules Committee met without public notice — a meeting that was almost certainly illegal — in the office of House Speaker Bobby Harrell (R-Charleston).

Rules Committee Chairman Converse Chellis (R-Summerville) notified only Republicans of the meeting, where they quickly hammered out a new rule to allow the GOP Caucus to meet behind closed doors in the Statehouse. And, of course, it passed the committee on a 10-1 vote. The rule change had not been publicly introduced or circulated in advance, as such changes usually are.

The rules change was hustled to the floor of the House, where members had only minutes to look it over before voting on it. Democrats tried vainly to delay the vote to allow discussion and public input. Republican leaders would not be deterred, though

10 Republicans apparently had enough sense of shame to vote against this shabby piece of business.

And, just like that, it was done. Final vote: 59-52.

Now Republicans in the General Assembly will be able to go behind closed doors and do — well, do just about any damned thing they want to do because there will be no press or public there to watch them.

"There is still a place in the world for political parties," said House Republican Caucus Leader Jim Merrill, of Daniel Island.

"Caucuses ought to be able to discuss strategy and how they are going to deal with the other side of the aisle as a group," Harrell said.

Others questioned the legality of the new GOP rules change, including Bill Rogers, executive director of the South Carolina Press Association, and Jay Bender, an attorney and expert on the state's Freedom of Information Act.

Both *The State* newspaper in Columbia and The *Post and Courier* editorialized against this legislative coup.

Wrote *The State*: "...the House added insult to this grievous injury to the people of South Carolina by effectively shutting the public out of what should have been a debate over these new rules to shut the public out of future debates."

The *P&C* said: "No doubt there's a place for political backroom talk — party headquarters. Once caucuses are made part of the government process, they should obey all the rules."

Nationwide, voters rose up and punished congressional Republicans for the way they had corrupted the legislative process. But nothing like that will happen in South Carolina, because in this state the Republicans are the White People's Party and white people would rather vote for corrupt Republicans than honest Democrats. And that's the difference between a healthy democracy and South Carolina.

January 31, 2007

REMEMBERING HARRY DENT
HE CHANGED THE WINDOW DRESSING OF SOUTH CAROLINA POLITICS

Harry Dent died on September 28. He was 77. If you don't recognize the name, that's understandable. Yet few people did more than Dent to usher the era of Republican dominance into South Carolina — and by extension, the South.

Today, the late Gov. Carroll Campbell and his flamboyant, self-promoting sidekick Lee Atwater get most of the credit for building the Republican Party in the Palmetto State, but before Campbell and Atwater, there was Dent. Probably no one more personified the nexus of race, religion, and Republicanism than the quiet, behind-the-scenes operator from Calhoun County. Anyone who doubts that the modern Republican Party is built on a foundation of racism should study his life and career.

Dent joined the staff of newly elected Sen. Strom Thurmond in 1955, only seven years after Thurmond had run for president on the Dixiecrat ticket, establishing himself as the nation's foremost segregationist. Within a year he was chief of staff.

In 1964, the national Democrats, led by President Lyndon Johnson, passed the Civil Rights Act, inflaming white Southerners and giving the Republicans the chance they had been looking for to break into the old Democratic South. More than anyone else, it was Dent who whispered into Thurmond's ear and said it was time to switch parties and become a Republican. That year Thurmond and Dent campaigned for Barry Goldwater, the GOP presidential candidate, using the code words of "states' rights" to denounce civil rights legislation and the federal government in terms white Southerners could understand without using the N-word. Goldwater carried South Carolina and four other southern states that year, and the Republican Party has ruled the South ever since.

In 1966, Dent worked hard in the off-year campaigns for state Republican candidates, helping to elect 26 of them to the General Assembly. It would take three more decades, but the GOP was on its way to taking control of the state legislature.

At the Republican national convention in Miami in 1968, Dent and Thurmond held the line on Southern delegates who wanted to bolt to Ronald Reagan, thus assuring that Richard Nixon received the nomination. In the general election, Dent and Thurmond worked hard to get white Southerners to support Nixon, rather than the third-party insurgency of segregationist George Wallace. In this campaign Dent became the architect of what was known as Nixon's "Southern strategy," whereby he reassured white Southerners that, as president, Nixon would go slow on civil rights issues, including school bussing. The strategy worked; Wallace carried five Deep South states, but most of the region held firm for Nixon, giving him the narrowest of margins over Hubert H. Humphrey.

In its notice on the death of Harry Dent, *The New York Times* wrote of his Southern strategy that, "Its detractors call it racism cloaked in code words like 'law and order'.... In any event, the strategy was credited with the Nixon victory."

After the election, Dent was rewarded with a position on the White House staff. There he met evangelist Billy Graham, who requested that he inaugurate a White House prayer breakfast. Dent complied, and the tradition continues nearly 40 years later, a precursor to the rampant religiosity which has suffused Washington politics in recent years.

In his last years, Dent walked away from politics and went into full-time evangelism, working closely with the Billy Graham Crusade and serving a hitch as a missionary to Romania.

As a reporter for *The State* newspaper, I met him a couple of times in that period. I think Dent took his religion seriously — certainly more seriously than most politicians, but it should be said that he helped open the gates of the modern GOP to the Christofascists who have grown so powerful in that party today. Likewise, I don't think he was a racist, but he pandered to them and gave them cover and respectability. That's an ugly legacy, but one which he shares with the other giants of the state Republican pantheon — Strom Thurmond, Carroll Campbell, and Lee Atwater.

In the final analysis, generations of political opportunists like

Dent have held the South back, have kept it stuck with two wheels in the ditch and its soul in purgatory. When the South needed moral leaders to confront its segregationist past, it got fixers and operators like Dent, who helped preserve and justify that segregation.

Harry Dent used to say that he just wanted to make South Carolina into a two-party state. The irony, of course, is that it is almost as much a one-party state today as it was a half-century ago. And that same party runs the state today — the White People's Party. Ultimately, Dent will be remembered for his role in helping that party change its name from Democratic to Republican.

October 7, 2007

WASN'T ONE GEORGE W. BUSH ENOUGH?
MARK SANFORD AIMS FOR 2012

"Let me tell you about the very rich," F. Scott Fitzgerald wrote. "They are different from you and me."

You bet your ass they are. And they like it that way.

They build prep schools, country clubs, and gated communities to keep the right attitudes in and the wrong people out. But most importantly, I think, they create these institutions and edifices to protect themselves from the consequences of their behavior.

If they do not see poverty, hunger, ignorance, and squalor, they can pretend these conditions are unconnected to them. They can dwell in their Reaganesque utopia of "invisible hands" and tides lifting boats. They can tell themselves that anybody with a little pluck and luck can make it to the top. They can point to themselves as proof of this timeless cliche.

What these plutocrats refuse to understand is that some people are simply born with more opportunities than others, with more doors to choose from, more presents to unwrap. And when their wits fail them or the economy falters, they will not land on the street. They will not sleep in a homeless shelter or stand in a morning labor pool, waiting for their names to be called. They will always have safety nets and cushions.

The United States in the twenty-first century is the most rigidly stratified society among Western industrialized democracies. If you are born poor in America, you will almost certainly die poor. And if you are born rich, it is almost impossible to become poor. In fact, it is possible to fail so frequently and so spectacularly that you eventually rise to the presidency of the United States.

As proof, I give you George W. Bush, a creature of privilege and presumption, arrogance and ignorance, a man who could have been produced only by an insular and degenerate plutocracy.

In South Carolina we have a man who aspires to be our next George W. Bush — Mark Sanford.

Gov. Sanford also comes from a background of privilege and presumption, and that worldview has produced a similar effect on his philosophy and politics.

Sanford was a wealthy man before he married Jenny Sullivan, an industrial heiress and Wall Street executive. The Sanfords made their home on Sullivan's Island, with a 98.74 percent white population and a median family income of $98,455, according to the 2000 census. Two years ago, *Forbes magazine* ranked the tony barrier island the 70th priciest zip code in the nation, based on real estate values. The Sanfords' house recently went on the market for $3.5 million. Since he was elected governor, Sanford's four sons have been enrolled at the exclusive Heathwood Hall Episcopal School in Columbia, where tuitions for K-12 range from $12,140 to $14,400 a year.

In this strange little parallel universe of violence, paranoia, and surrealism called South Carolina, anything can happen. In recent months the world has been amused at the sight of our governor trying to turn down $700 million in federal stimulus money from Washington. Last fall he dithered and pontificated over accepting money to pay for food stamps and unemployment compensation. In the state with the second-highest unemployment rate in the nation, Sanford preached his tired old libertarian, free-market ideology while 77,000 unemployed South Carolinians waited in despair.

Sanford eventually gave in on the unemployment compensation funds, but now he is turning his back on the stimulus money targeted for education and law enforcement. Without the federal money, up to 2,600 public school employees, including 1,500 teachers, will lose their jobs, along with SLED agents and prison guards. Hundreds of convicts may have to be released early.

Sanford has won rebuke far and wide for his latest posturing, including in the pages of *The New York Times* and *The Post and Courier*. But there are two things you need to understand: First, Sanford's decisions won't affect him or his family. His children go to private school. He lives in the Governor's Mansion and works in the Statehouse, two of the most tightly guarded venues in the state. He has nothing to fear from muggers or burglars. He is rich, and he is safe from the consequences of his behavior. And second, he is playing to a wider audience. Mark Sanford has not ruled out running for president in 2012, and he is building his reputation among some conservatives as a libertarian true believer. And it seems to be working. He is getting good reviews in some quarters of the Republican Party.

Frankly, I would like to see Sanford win the Republican nomination in 2012. Then he could do to the Republican Party what the Republicans did to the American economy.

April 15, 2009

IN THEIR OWN WORDS
DEMINT'S FOLLOWERS GIVE INSIGHT INTO THE GOP MINDSET

"If we're able to stop Obama on this, it will be his Waterloo. It will break him."

—Sen. Jim DeMint

Yes, you've read it. We've all read it. South Carolina's junior senator is on the warpath against President Barack Obama and healthcare reform. He's clearly scoring points with the yahoo contingent of the Republican Party. That's good for Jim DeMint and for yahoos, but does it do the GOP any good?

Post and Courier columnist Brian Hicks took up this issue last week and reached a conclusion I am not sure I agree with: ""These days, the South is a mirror of the nation, a state of mind. Geography has little to do with it."

Granted, there are yahoos — even full-blooded rednecks — in other parts of the nation. Joe the Plumber and Sarah Palin might have just as easily come from Dorchester County. But they are the exceptions that prove my point.

As the Republican Party shrinks in numbers and demographics, what is left tends to be old, white, religious, and crazy as a June bug. And we have more of those in the South than anywhere else. That's why the South is the reddest region of the country and it's why Jim DeMint and other extremists will keep throwing red meat to these true believers. He's got nothing to lose. As the Republican Party grows smaller and angrier, DeMint's stature within it will only rise.

I started thinking of this recently after a friend suggested I go to DeMint's blog at jimdemint.com/blog/2009/07 and see what his followers are saying to their hero in the "intimacy" of a blog. There they swear their love and fealty to DeMint; they pour out their anger and fears — mostly fears. White Southerners are nothing if not fearful. Fear has been driving their politics and culture for 200 years and generations of politicians have been happy to stoke their fears with incendiary rhetoric.

In the past, those fears have been about race and communism; today they are about socialism and healthcare reform. White Southerners have always seen the world as hostile, full of dark and insidious forces, usually emanating from Washington, Moscow, or the United Nations.

DeMint's fans and followers describe current issues in nothing less than apocalyptic terms. One of them writes: Democrats "are ruining this fine country with their Socialist policies and government takeover tactics. I firmly believe that the Democratic Party is in the process of destroying The Constitution and stripping us of our rights."

And another: "I think Obama has one goal in mind and that is to destroy our civil and political system as it has existed and made this country the best that has ever existed. Obama will be happy when we are all subserviant [sic] to the totaliarian [sic] government as is the world and faith of his family."

Read this one and you can almost hear the black helicopters circling overhead: "OBAMA is POWER HUNGER[sic] ... It seems more clear every day that his plan for CHANGE is to ignore the U.S. Constitution and convert the office of president to DICTATOR ... By then he will have merged us with Canada and Mexico to form the North American Union which he can deliver to the United Nations."

Among the senator's correspondents there is much referencing of the Almighty and many wishes of "God bless you." There is no question among DeMint's supporters that god is on their side.

"I am praying for you, and that God would stop Obama's agenda sometime," wrote one inspired supporter. "Thank you for being His tool. I am proud to have you representing my state in Washington! ... God bless you!"

In response to Sen. DeMint's remark, President Obama said, "This is not about me." For many of the president's critics, it clearly is about him.

"At this point in the Obama Administration, I wouldn't believe Obama if he told me he was black..." one wrote. "I've never witness [sic] such decite [sic] as this person puts forth.... WHERE IS THE BIRTH CERTIFICATE...????????????????????? THAT IS THE SINGLE BIGGEST ISSUE, and everyone of you should be DEMANDING it be brought out in the Sun Light..."

Another wrote: "I think that Obama and company don't have a plan, they've got an agenda ... They and the rest of the Democrats (Socialists) think we're a lot of 'Clueless Serfs.' They're a lot of hypocrites. And Obama (I refuse to call him President) is a serial liar to boot!!!"

Go to DeMint's blog and read for yourself what the party of Lincoln, Teddy Roosevelt, and Eisenhower sounds like in the 21st century. This is not the voice of reason or the voice of compassion. But it is the voice of President Obama's "loyal opposition" in governing this country.

August 5, 2009

WHAT DOES THE GOP REALLY WANT?
IF HENRY MCMASTER IS ANY INDICATION, THEY REALLY DON'T KNOW

The strange Republican coalition of corporate interests and cultural conservatism, which has dominated American politics for most of the last half-century, seems to be coming unraveled.

The various factions and sub-factions within this contrived alliance barely understand one another, and when they try to speak at once, the cacophony is incomprehensible.

The corporate and religious wings of the GOP have been at cross purposes for years. Not as clear to most observers are the fissures within the respective wings of the party. For example, on the "family values" side, cultural conservatives have long argued that working mothers should stay at home and welfare mothers should get a job.

On the question of abortion, religious conservatives would force every woman to carry her pregnancy to term, regardless of whether she wants or can afford to keep the child, and whether she is intellectually and emotionally capable of raising a child.

But what becomes of the child after it is born? Here protectors of the unborn run headlong into libertarian fanatics who say that the government has no business raising people's children or even educating them. This philosophical dichotomy helps explain the appalling levels of childhood poverty, malnutrition, dropout rates, and other pathologies in this country.

Something like that has been happening on the corporate side of the coalition, as well, with equally dire consequences for public policy.

For decades the GOP ideology has been dominated by the double mantra, deregulation and tort reform. In this deregulated environment, we have seen a flood of faulty and dangerous goods and services in the market — everything from credit default swaps to food tainted with E.coli and toys tainted with lead paint.

Faced with a government that has refused to do its job to protect consumers from corporate predators, many people have concluded that their only defense it to sue the bastards. And that's where tort reform comes in. Those same corporate sponsors who put the Republicans in power and incited them to deregulate banking and industry have also been lobbying to make it more difficult for citizens to sue those financial institutions and manufacturers.

Against this backdrop, we are seeing some strange behavior on the part of S.C. Attorney General Henry McMaster. Two weeks ago, McMaster's office won a $45 million lawsuit against pharmaceutical giant Eli Lilly in a case involving improper marketing and distribution of the anti-psychotic drug Zyprexa.

Let me say that again. GOP warhorse Henry McMaster, who has been long and loud in his call for tort reform, took the big pill pusher to court and stuck it to them for $45 million! And he is crowing about it to all who will listen. And why not? As a candidate in next year's GOP gubernatorial primary, McMaster needs all the good press he can get.

At issue was Lilly's marketing of Zyprexa for unapproved "off-label" uses, such as pediatric applications and treatment of depression. It is illegal to market a drug for off-label uses or pay for off-label prescriptions with federal Medicaid money. According to *The Post and Courier*, the AG's suit also claimed that Lilly failed to warn Zyprexa users of potentially dangerous side effects, including diabetes and heart problems.

It is good that Lilly was brought to account on this matter. But the issue does raise some interesting questions about Republicans, litigation, and individual rights.

Henry McMaster does not want you or me to be able to sue companies like Eli Lilly, which makes me wonder why he is so eager to do it himself in the name of the state.

To answer that question, I left a message with Mark Plowden, spokesman for the AG's office, but got no response. So I was left to my own devices to answer my question in the manner of a good GOPer: Only somebody with the wisdom and resources of the attorney general should be allowed to sue corporations. We can't allow just anyone to run around suing companies willy-nilly, now can we?

But wait a minute, I say to myself. Isn't it another plank of conservative ideology that individuals should take care of themselves and government should get out of the way? Shouldn't a person who has been hurt by an incompetent doctor or a corrupt corporation have legal recourse? Access to the courts is as fundamental to freedom as the right to bear arms, and it is just as important in the individual's defense of his person, home, and family. How does Henry McMaster feel about those values?

The Republican "philosophy" is a grab bag of greed, superstition, and reckless opportunism, and it has been a public policy disaster for this nation. But the bag is coming unraveled, and we are coming to see these ugly behaviors for what they are. It's about time.

November 4, 2009

CLOWNS AND DANCING BEARS
HENRY BROWN BRINGS THE CIRCUS TO THE 1ST DISTRICT

Nobody — least of all Rep. Henry Brown — could have guessed what an unholy shit storm he would unleash when he announced in January that he would not seek a sixth term representing the 1st Congressional District.

This is one of those stories that just gets weirder and weirder every week, and it is many weeks from being over. It is a story that demonstrates the pathology and futility of South Carolina politics as clearly as anything could.

Let's start with Brown himself, a professional politician with 25 years on the public payroll. It is hard to imagine a less remarkable, more mediocre man. During 10 years in Congress, he accomplished nothing memorable except to serve as a rubber stamp to George W. Bush's wars, tax cuts, and record budget deficits. If you could find 10 people on the street who recognized the name "Henry Brown" and asked them what they knew about him, the majority would probably recall that it was Brown who set a controlled burn on his farm in Berkeley County in 2004. The fire jumped the property line into the Francis Marion National Forest, burning 20 acres of public land. Brown then used his congressional muscle to squelch a National Forest Service fine.

In 2008, Brown won re-election with only 52 percent of the vote against Democrat Linda Ketner. The man was clearly vulnerable and had become a GOP liability. When the 74-year-old politician released a statement in January saying he wanted to get out of Washington and spend more time at his farm, it sounded plausible enough. Then all hell broke loose.

Republicans started coming out of the woodwork to make their bids for Brown's job. So far, 10 have declared their intentions, and, with another week to go before the filing deadline, there's still time for one or two more. (There are also three Democrats and one Independent Party candidate in the race.)

I will not name all of the hungry GOPers here. Let it suffice to say that I never heard of several of them, and half have never held public office. Three of them do bear mentioning, though. Carroll "Tumpy" Campbell is the son of the late GOP governor of the same name. Paul Thurmond is the son of the late U.S. Sen. Strom Thurmond. And state Rep. Tim Scott enjoys the questionable distinction of being the first black Republican to sit in the General Assembly since Reconstruction. One of these three will almost certainly be our next congressman.

At the time of their announcements, several of the candidates made a point of saying their first priority would be to cut taxes. And most tried to claim the title of "true conservative" in the race.

Ah, yes. The true conservative. In this most conservative of states, the first thing a Republican must do is prove that he is more conservative than his rivals. He must demonstrate that he is angrier and more intolerant, more indifferent to suffering and injustice, more scornful of science and academe. He must prove that he loves Jesus, his wife, and Ronald Reagan, and he must do it all while paying homage to the Second Amendment and the power of the free market.

Of course, the danger for the true conservative is that enthusiasm might overwhelm judgment. That's apparently what happened a few weeks ago when gubernatorial candidate Andre Bauer — in an effort to demonstrate that he despises poor people more than his GOP rivals — compared the poor to stray animals. It is notable that, while nobody in his Republican audience objected to the remark, Bauer was called out and ridiculed from sea to shining sea. Within days he was apologizing and explaining and receiving special recognition on *The Daily Show*.

Now imagine what 10 Republicans are going to do when turned loose in the same pen leading up to the June primary. Ten desperate GOPers, each trying to be more conservative than the others, each edging farther and farther to the right, trying not to fall off the edge like brother Andre. One of them is sure to say something really stupid, really offensive. What will it be? A call for mandatory school prayer? A call to execute homosexuals?

Whatever, we've got 10 weeks to watch and wait, as the late-night comics anticipate more manna from South Carolina.

And in the latest twist, Henry Brown, the man who set this round of musical chairs in motion, declared recently that he is running for the job of supervisor of Berkeley County against his old friend Dan Davis. Apparently Henry wasn't so eager to retire after all.

Which leads us to wonder who may have put the screws to him to leave Washington. Regardless, it's going to be another ugly GOP race in a really weird year.

March 24, 2010

THE POLITICS OF BLACK AND WHITE
IN THIS STATE, YOU CAN'T UNDERSTAND ANYTHING WITHOUT RACE

This state's tragic racial history weaves itself through our culture in complex, sometimes ironic ways. But whatever form it takes, it is always poison, and it paralyzes our social and economic development like a scorpion's sting paralyzes its victims.

We saw this tragedy in all its ugly permutations last week, when Republican and Democratic candidates for governor held their respective debates, Democrats on May 2, Republicans the following night. Let's begin with the GOPers.

The Republican Party in the South — a.k.a. the White People's Party — has been the bulwark of segregation and social reaction for more than 40 years. Party leaders have used racial rhetoric and code — such as the Confederate flag and welfare — to keep the majority of whites in the GOP tent and voting against their own interests. The GOP has used its power at the polls to push programs detrimental to public education, the environment, and economic and social justice.

We got a glimpse of all this when Republican candidates Lt. Gov. André Bauer, U.S. Rep. Gresham Barrett, state Rep. Nikki

Haley, and Attorney General Henry McMaster faced off on SC ETV last week. In response to questions from moderator Mark Quinn, the four lined up shoulder-to-shoulder in support of Arizona's draconian new immigration law. This was a red-meat issue that would allow no nuance or equivocation. Bauer trumped them all, however, by riffing on his earlier theme that giving welfare to poor people was like feeding stray animals. But now he says that giving welfare to illegal immigrants encourages illegal immigration. Does he not know that welfare for illegals is against the law, or does he just assume we are too stupid to call him on it?

The candidates also agreed they would veto any attempt to raise the state's lowest-in-the-nation, seven-cent cigarette tax. Keeping taxes at rock bottom is more important than raising money for indigent healthcare or preventing young people from taking up smoking — the two most commonly cited justifications for raising the nicotine tax.

Taxes were at the heart of the gubernatorial debate, taking up half of the event's 56 minutes. McMaster said he wanted flatter taxes, a line that must have warmed the hearts of his wealthy family and patrons. In a state with one of the widest disparities of wealth in the nation, it takes chutzpah to call for flatter taxes. But among Republican true believers, a flat tax has been the Holy Grail since the Reagan years. McMaster knew exactly who he was talking to.

McMaster, Haley, and Bauer said they favored the elimination of all corporate income taxes.

"If we really want to change the way that South Carolina is perceived, that would be the number one vehicle," Bauer said. "Businesses would flock here. They'd come here solely based on the (elimination of the corporate) income tax."

McMaster said, "I want to make this the most business-friendly state in the country." None of the candidates said anything about making this the best educated state or the safest or the cleanest state in the country. Just the most business-friendly.

Of course, South Carolina already has one of the lowest corporate tax rates in the nation. If that was all business wanted from us, we would be among the most industrialized states. But businesses are looking for an educated work force, sound infrastructure, and a safe and livable environment — all things that cost money. But you heard hardly a word last Monday night about these issues. The whole discussion of education was wrapped up in less than eight minutes. And speaking of the environment, all four GOP candidates were still enthusiastic about drilling for oil and natural gas in South Carolina waters, less than two weeks after the cataclysmic spill in the Gulf of Mexico.

In short, this quartet was clearly serenading a well-healed white constituency with just enough red-meat talk about illegal immigrants and welfare cheats to bring the god-and-guns crowd along. It has worked for the Republicans for 40 years, and it worked for the Democrats before the great party realignment. It will probably work in 2010.

After eight years of failure and scandal, which has left this state in the worst economic mess it has known in decades, shouldn't South Carolina be ready for a change? Yet the white people of this state are going to return Republican majorities to the House and Senate and probably put another GOPer in the governor's mansion. They can't help themselves. And that is the tragedy of South Carolina, a state trapped in its racial past like a mammoth in a tar pit.

May 12, 2010

THE POWER OF IGNORANCE
IT'S WHAT DRIVES SOUTH CAROLINA'S POLITICAL CULTURE

It's times like these that make me suspect that South Carolina Republicans underfund the state's public schools with the malicious intent of keeping people too ignorant to understand what the hell is going on.

Want some proof? On the heals of December's Secession Gala, in which grown men and women dressed up in Confederate costumes and strutted about the Gaillard Auditorium, the Stephen Dill Lee Institute — described by *The Post and Courier* as "something of a Confederate think-tank formed by the Sons of Confederate Veterans" — hosted a downtown conference under the name "Lincoln vs. Jefferson: Opposing Visions of America."

I did not attend this little shindig, in part because I refused to shell out the $150 admission, but also because I had a pretty good idea what the conclusions of the participants would be. When the SCV starts talking about Abraham Lincoln, you don't have to be a weatherman to know which way the wind is blowing.

And in case there was any doubt, a SCV spokesman spelled it out: "Jefferson was a proponent of decentralized government, while Lincoln was for big government and high taxes."

Ah, yes. Big government and high taxes, those bugaboos of conservatives and white Southerners, two groups which are pretty much synonymous.

But what conservatives cannot understand — or choose to ignore — is that political power cannot be created or destroyed. It can only be moved around.

The Founders of the Republic sought to balance that power between the states and the federal government. Thomas Jefferson — the hero of the neo-Confederates — dreamed of a bucolic, idyllic yeoman's republic, in which citizens (white, of course) lived in relative equality on their own farms, traded in the local economy, and were barely touched by outside commerce or federal authority. Good theory, but Jefferson's vision was never more than a fantasy.

153

The ink wasn't dry on the Constitution before the Industrial Revolution exploded on the North American continent and transformed the new nation. The driving force behind that transformation was the privately held corporation.

The Founders could never have imagined the magnitude of modern corporations, some of which are larger than the economies of whole nations. They could never have imagined the influence these behemoths would exercise over our society, our economy, and our environment. If they had, I like to think they would have designed their Constitution very differently.

To repeat: Political power cannot be created or destroyed. It can only be moved around.

Corporations have accrued such power in recent decades that they collectively have become the most powerful force in America. And yet there is scant recognition of them in the Constitution.

For all their benefactions, corporations corrupt our political system, despoil our environment, send our jobs overseas, and crash our markets. And the only authority with any hope of checking or balancing this undemocratic, multinational power is the federal government. It is the federal government that has created the most effective laws to protect the nation's environment; regulate its banking, finance, and insurance industries; enforce safety standards for its food and drugs; establish rules for resolving labor-management disputes; provide healthcare for all; and so much more.

The federal government does these things because the states are physically and legally powerless to regulate the likes of Ford, BP, Dow Chemical, Bank of America, Kraft Foods, and Southwest Airlines. These corporations must be held to some level of accountability. Trust and dependability are the pillars of a modern industrial democracy. Federal law and regulation are the only things that keep giant corporations from grinding all of us under their heel. And the Feds haven't been doing such a good job lately. Behold the wreck Wall Street made of our economy two years ago.

What is amazing to the outsider and the educated person is the way white South Carolinians are constantly denouncing the federal government, its laws, and the taxes necessary to support it. They just can't get past that Civil War thing. A century and a half later, the federal government is still the enemy.

On Election Day, white South Carolinians voted overwhelmingly against the right of workers to organize, going against Washington's wishes. And South Carolina is considering becoming the first state to withdraw from the federal Medicaid program. Last week Sen. Lindsey Graham announced that he would introduce legislation to exempt the state from participating in the new healthcare reform law. He did not explain how we were supposed to take care of the 40 percent of our people who are uninsured. The list of such follies would fill volumes.

Regulation follows technology and commerce with the certainty of gravity. To acknowledge that simple fact would transform South Carolina's politics and culture. No wonder our politicians don't want us to know it.

February 9, 2011

THE ARROGANCE OF THE SC GOP
REPUBLICANS HAVE MORE JOB SECURITY THAN ANY UNION

Ultimately, we get the government we deserve. The cynicism with which white people go to the polls and vote Republican in this state is matched only by the cynicism with which those elected Republicans betray the voters who put them in office. The Nikki Haley administration is barely two months old and the pattern is clearly repeating itself.

Mark Sanford was the most recent GOP wonder boy, twice elected governor with overwhelming majorities. He mouthed the Republican platitudes of small government, low taxes, and family values. But as the world knows, he also had a mistress in Argentina, and he abandoned his office and his state to visit her there in 2009 while lying about his whereabouts and authorizing no one to act for him in event of an emergency.

When the ruse was exposed, both the governor and the state were reduced to punch lines in the national media. Yet the GOP-dominated General Assembly took only the mild measure of censuring him; no serious effort was made to remove him from office. It has been suggested that one reason the solons did not bring impeachment charges against Sanford was that the person in line to replace him was Lt. Gov. André Bauer, an amazingly callow and self-indulgent young man, now remembered primarily for his reckless driving and flying.

But the white people of South Carolina demonstrated that they had learned nothing from the experience. They were ready to elect to the highest offices in the state anyone who recited the GOP mantra of small government and low taxes. And so they elected Republicans down the line, putting GOPers in all nine statewide executive offices and extending the Republican majority to more than 60 percent of the General Assembly. Most significantly to many observers, they turned out 28-year congressional veteran John Spratt from his House District 5 seat, replacing him with a York County real estate developer who had a record of sleazy and questionable dealings. Spratt was chairman of the powerful House Committee on the Budget and one of the most respected members of Congress. But he was a Democrat, and that wasn't good enough for the white folks of South Carolina.

Now, we have Gov. Nikki Haley. Even before she was elected, there were serious questions about her marital fidelity and her business practices. But when Sarah Palin swept into town to anoint her at a rally on the steps of the Statehouse, white people got the message. They gave her the gubernatorial nomination over four male opponents and elected her governor over an appealing and moderate young Democrat. Palin's own ethical and intellectual failings were never an issue for the majority of white voters.

Since taking office, Haley has already found herself in two messy pieces of business. Columbia journalists obtained Haley's application for employment from her last job and tax records from the job prior to that. In applying for the new job at Lexington Medical Center, she claimed to be making $125,000 a year at her old job and expected as much at Lexington Medical. In fact, tax records showed she claimed only $22,000 a year in that previous job.

Was this a crime? No. An impeachable offense? Hardly. But it does say something about her character, and if she was hiding income from the IRS, she might have much bigger problems.

More recently, she removed from the University of South Carolina Board of Trustees Darla Moore, the greatest benefactor in the history of the school, having given $70 million over the years. She replaced Moore with a friend who had donated $4,500 to her gubernatorial campaign. Her only explanation was that she wanted "fresh eyes" on the board.

Again, nothing criminal or impeachable, but the behavior certainly puts Haley's judgment in question. So far the General Assembly has no reason to consider removing her, but if it should, who is standing by to replace her?

Lt. Gov. Ken Ard was elected overwhelmingly last November in the GOP sweep. He brought little experience to the job: two terms on Florence County Council. But he has brought a lot of baggage.

The Associated Press reports that the state Ethics Commission has accused Ard of 106 ethics violations, including using campaign funds to pay personal expenses. Ard has hired an attorney.

His friends and former colleagues in Florence County defend his integrity, saying any shortcomings were errors and oversights, but it should make reasonable people wonder if a man who could not run his campaign for lieutenant governor is ready to run the office of lieutenant governor — or the office above that.

But the white people of South Carolina are not losing any sleep over this question. They know there is a Republican in office, and that is all they want to know. Any further information would be irrelevant.

March 30, 2011

(Ken Ard pleaded guilty to multiple ethics violations and resigned the office of lieutenant governor in March 2012.)

THE REPUBLICAN CREED
A LICENSE FOR GREED AND IRRESPONSIBILITY

"I do not choose to be a common man. It is my right to be uncommon. If I can seek opportunity, not security, I want to take the calculated risk to dream and to build, to fail and to succeed. I refuse to barter incentive for dole. I prefer the challenges of life to guaranteed security, the thrill of fulfillment to the state of calm utopia. I will not trade freedom for beneficence, nor my dignity for a handout. I will never cower before any master, save my God. It is my heritage to stand erect, proud, and unafraid: to think and act for myself, enjoy the benefit of my creations, and to face the whole world boldly and say, 'I am a free American.'"

— Republican Creed

If you were not aware that the Republican Party has a creed, you are not alone. I don't generally hang around with Republicans in large numbers, and the thought of hearing a roomful of GOPers reciting this maxim in unison puts chills on the back of my neck. But a friend of mine attended a recent GOP meeting and heard the recitation. A copy of the creed was printed on the back of the meeting program for the benefit of those who had not committed it to memory. As he later told me, "This could have been written by Ayn Rand."

Yes, I guess it could have, now that I think of it. But what first struck me was that little of this creed describes the actual Republicans I know and hear about. Most of those GOPers have little in common with the almost Nietzschean Übermensch represented by these words. The Republicans I know are rather plain little people who live in their plain little houses and go to their plain little jobs, all of which are designed to protect them from the vagaries of a rambunctious economic system and from the social and cultural nonconformity inherent in a free society.

Indeed, much of the energy of the modern Republican Party comes from their fervor to ban and punish behavior they find offensive. In earlier decades, GOPers were closely associated with loyalty oaths and with the anticommunist hysteria of Joe McCarthy and Richard Nixon. They have brought their hysteria into the twenty-first century with their anti-terrorist fury and their acceptance of warrantless wiretaps and "enhanced interrogation." Fear is the glue that holds the Republican Party together.

What I do not see in this creed is any aspiration to excellence of mind or character. The GOP has become the party of anti-intellectualism and anti-scientific thought. Leaders like Jim DeMint and Sarah Palin use the blunt instrument of populist rage against what they term "elitism." What could be more at odds with the spirit of the "uncommon man"?

Nor do I see in this Republican statement any affirmation of community, any acknowledgment that other human beings are part of this society in which the Republican lives and a part of this economy with which he is so deeply enthralled. Anyone who can recite this creed has clearly come a long way from the patriotism of John F. Kennedy, who told his fellow Americans, "Ask not what your country can do for you. Ask what you can do for your country."

Also missing in this creed is any acknowledgment of a responsibility to our living environment. I know that it is religiosity that keeps many Republicans focused on the hereafter, completely ignoring any obligation to the biosphere in which their children and grandchildren will some day live. But increasingly, this anti-environmentalism seems to be ideological. Talk to a Libertarian or "small government" Republican, and he will have glib and easy answers to almost any problem facing the country today. The solution, he will tell you, is less government, more economic growth, more privatization, more individual responsibility. It all sounds so reasonable, so plausible, until you come to the great conundrum no conservative has satisfactorily addressed: How do we protect our environment?

Here the conservative's cool rationalism turns to simplemindedness or evasion. Somehow the environment will protect itself, he says. Somehow anyone dumping anything into the air and water in the pursuit of profit will make a better world for all of us.

What about the greatest threat facing the world today?

What about global climate change? The Republican has a simple answer: There is no climate change.

The denial of climate change, like the denial of evolution and other scientific certainties, is part of the Republican ideology. I'm surprised it is not part of the Republican Creed. And as you read that creed more carefully, you realize that all the bold talk about opportunity, risk, incentive, and freedom is not an ode to human liberty, but a license for unbridled greed.

June 1, 2011

THE PRAYER BEFORE THE BOMB
THIS IS WHAT HAPPENS WHEN YOU DEAL WITH TERRORISTS

South Carolina politicians have a long history of embarrassing their state. If it's not Joe "You Lie" Wilson interrupting a joint session of Congress and insulting the president, it's Mark Sanford and his Argentine mistress or Strom Thurmond standing on his head for a *Life* magazine photographer or brawling with a Senate colleague in the halls of Congress.

Now we have the Praying Freshmen.

Five of the state's U.S. House delegation are Republicans, and four of them — including Charleston County's Tim Scott — are freshmen. They are all allied with the Tea Party. And they like to pray.

As the Associated Press reported during the recent debt ceiling debate, "Walking to the members' chapel alone, [2nd District] Rep. Jeff Duncan glanced at his phone and saw a text from fellow freshman [5th District] Rep. Mick Mulvaney, who told him to hang on — he would like to come too. Along the way Mulvaney found Rep. Tim Scott and brought him along."

With the Lord as their shepherd, they found the strength to join their fellow South Carolina GOPers, 1st District Rep. Joe Wilson and 4th District Rep. Trey Gowdy, in voting to lop huge chunks out of the federal budget in exchange for raising the debt ceiling.

Of course, there are cynics who suspect that the congressmen's prayers were less than sincere. One was Kathleen Parker, Pulitzer Prize-winning columnist, outspoken conservative, and South Carolinian, who was snarky enough to suggest that the freshmen GOPers were at least as much afraid of Sen. Jim DeMint as they were of the Almighty. She pointed out that the Tea Party senator had threatened to "primary" any congressman who did not toe the line and hold out for maximum budget cuts. These freshmen did not believe that god wanted them to be one-term representatives, so they did as god and DeMint commanded — not necessarily in that order.

I am also reminded of something Herb Silverman wrote recently. Silverman is South Carolina's leading atheist, founder of Secular Humanists of the Lowcountry and the Secular Coalition of America. In a recent online column for the *Washington Post*, he noted that the Almighty is quick to the aid of troubled politicians in this state. When former Gov. Mark Sanford was caught after his Appalachian Trail misadventure, many called for his resignation, but Sanford had a better idea. He prayed, and god told him to hang in there. In 2009, when Sen. DeMint was worried about running for re-election while his wife battled cancer, he too took it to the Lord in prayer, and — wouldn't you know it? — god told him to run. Looks like these congressional freshmen are taking a cue from the veteran prayer bosses in the state GOP.

What worries me is not that these freshmen seem to be cribbing out of Sanford's and DeMint's prayer book — maybe even stealing their password to the Almighty. No, what I find most troubling is how difficult it would be to carry out a rational and useful policy debate with these god GOPers. They could trump any fact, any argument, any line of reasoning by running off to the chapel, coming back a few minutes later and saying, "Just talked it over with god and the Big Guy says I'm right and you're wrong." End of argument.

For *New York Times* columnist Joe Nocera, it is a bigger question than whose side god is on. As he sees it, the Tea Party is against America.

"These last few months, much of the country has watched in horror as the Tea Party Republicans have waged jihad on the American people," he wrote. "Their intransigent demands for deep spending cuts, coupled with their almost gleeful willingness to destroy one of America's most invaluable assets, its full faith and credit, were incredibly irresponsible. But they didn't care. Their goal, they believed, was worth blowing up the country for, if that's what it took."

The tea baggers must have been taking their orders from god. They certainly were not taking them from the American people. Polls showed a wide majority of Americans were ready to raise taxes on the rich and opposed cuts to social programs.

Before they blow themselves up in public places, jihadists do what our congressmen do — they pray. Of course, the South Carolina jihadists and their tea-bag buddies did not blow themselves up. They blew up the United States economy — or threatened to.

The take-home message, as Nocera wrote, is clear enough: "Never negotiate with terrorists. It only encourages them."

We negotiated, and we got burned. Do not doubt that the Tea Party terrorists will be back with all their god talk, rage, threats, and self-righteousness. Will we be ready next time?

August 10, 2011

I COULDN'T MAKE THIS STUFF UP
SO HOW DOES RICK PERRY GET AWAY WITH IT?

Honestly, some weeks I don't even have to write this column. It just falls from the heavens like manna. I pick it up and post it. This was one of those weeks.

Rick Perry. The name alone is enough to elicit chuckles. Big hat. Silly boots. Cowboy swagger.

The Texas governor likes to hold stadium-sized prayer rallies in which he fills a fraction of the seats and talks to god. Two years ago he held a rally to ask god for rain. Today, Texas still bakes in a historic drought, suggesting that if there is a god, he's got better things to do than listen to Rick Perry. Three weeks ago Gov. Perry did it again, holding a prayer rally to save the nation's economy. Two days later, Dow Jones tanked more than 600 points, inspiring late-night comedians and TV pundits to suggest that Perry's prayers felt more like a curse.

When he is not talking to god, Perry is running his mouth to the craziest people in America, the tea baggers, and in 2009 he seemed to be flirting with secession — though the word never passed his lips. Two weeks ago he was in Charleston, the site of the original secession and the beginning of the Civil War, to declare his presidential intentions. Was this coincidence?

Coincidence or not, it has been like catnip to pundits and columnists. Writing in *U.S. News & World Report* Robert Schlesinger said, "And while talking about secession undoubtedly plays well among the three in 10 Texas voters ill-informed enough to think it's a serious political statement, it also makes the rest of the country (and likely the rest of the state) roll our eyes in bewilderment at the Lone Star Clown."

True enough, but Perry knows where his natural base is, and the Lone Star Clown is already planning a bus tour of the Palmetto State. I am confident he will get the welcome he came for. But what does that say about the people of South Carolina?

As I write this column, Gov. Perry has been a presidential candidate for less than a week, and he has already been caught in at least one screaming lie and one statement so outrageous that only a certified tea bagger — or South Carolina GOPer — could not be offended.

In one campaign stop he said he does not believe in man-made global climate change (as if his belief had anything to do with it) and went on to say that "hardly a day goes by" that some scientist is not caught faking data to support the global warming argument.

In fact, no scientist has been caught faking climate data and only the fools who live in the Fox News bubble could believe such a lie. But there are thousands of such people in this state, and they will be laying palmetto branches in front of Rick Perry's bus.

This is also a good place for Perry to repeat Mitt Romney's statement that "corporations are people" with all the rights of humans. In this right-to-work state with the lowest level of union membership in the nation, this will be music to the corporate culture. What it means for people is unclear.

It will be interesting to see if Perry challenges the patriotism of native son and Fed chief Ben Bernanke while he's here. Last week he said it would be "treacherous" if he tried "printing money" to deal with the current economic crisis. He seemed to be threatening Bernanke when he said "we would treat him pretty ugly down in Texas."

I'm sure this schoolyard tough talk will play well in South Carolina, but I am also confident that most Americans would like a little more subtlety, a little more dignity from a man who aspires to be our president.

Leno, Letterman, Maher, Fallon and the folks at *Saturday Night Live* would love to see Rick Perry in the White House. It would mean for them the same thing it means for me: years of free material. But leading the United States of America — leading it morally and politically — is serious business. I see no evidence that Gov. Perry is up to the task. And it is easy to understand why. There is little in the backward and parochial political culture of Texas that would prepare a person for running a huge and complex nation such as the United States.

Like his predecessor, George W. Bush, Perry already seems to be in over his head. He does not understand that more people are laughing at him than with him.

Perry's candidacy guarantees that we will have an exciting campaign — at least through the Republican National Convention. Let's hope it ends there.

August 24, 2011

ALL THE WORLD'S A STAGE
NEWT GINGRICH IS ABOUT TO MAKE HIS LAST EXIT

In South Carolina, we live for this quadrennial moment, the Republican presidential primary. Not since April 12, 1861, have so many eyes been on our little state. And this political event evokes many of the same passions as did the firing on Fort Sumter a century and a half ago.

I am not going to put South Carolina on the couch in this column. I have been doing that for years, and I think my sanity has been more damaged by the therapy than this state's has been repaired.

But there is one sick soul I would like to analyze at this moment: Newt Gingrich. I have been following the former Speaker of the House with a mixture of amusement and horror for more than two decades. It was Gingrich, and his infamous GOPAC training films and memos, who did more to create the polarization and acrimony that dominate today's political climate than any other individual.

He led the GOP revolution that took over the U.S. House in 1994 by railing against the "corruption" of the Democratic Party. Yet, by the time he was forced out of the speakership four years later, he had been fined $300,000 by the House Ethics Committee for his own transgressions.

Newt Gingrich has an ego that is truly frightening. He has

called himself a "transformative historical figure" and said, "People like me are what stands between us and Auschwitz."

Being out of office for more than a decade, he now casts himself in the image of Lincoln and Churchill, two politicians who were defeated and left to "wander in the wilderness," until destiny called them back in the hour of crisis.

Driven by such delusions, he now finds himself effectively out of the running for the GOP nomination following major losses in the Iowa caucuses and the New Hampshire primary. After peaking in the polls last month, his surge collapsed under a savage barrage of TV ads from the Mitt Romney campaign and its allied Super PACs. Now as Gingrich begins to see the bleak end of his checkered career, we get a look inside the dark mind of the man who would be our leader.

Gingrich knows that he will never be president. He has that much grasp on reality, but he has determined that he will not let Romney be president, either. In what some have called a kamikaze campaign, he has launched his own TV blitzkrieg against the former Massachusetts governor here in the Palmetto State. Curiously, he has chosen to attack Romney for what many are calling "vulture capitalism."

As founder and head of Bain Capital, Romney oversaw the buying, restructuring, and sometimes liquidation of numerous companies. Whether the companies were saved or not, Romney and his Bain directors and shareholders always had a big payday. Over the years, Romney and his friends destroyed thousands of jobs and Romney personally pocketed an estimated $250 million. It was a grubby business and Romney undoubtedly expected it would be an issue during the campaign. What he did not expect was that a fellow Republican would be the one bringing it up.

As I write this, 10 days before the South Carolina primary, Gingrich is promising to unleash a 30-minute "documentary" exposing Romney and Bain Capital. Republican leaders are warning him to back off, lest he become a pariah in his own party. At this writing there is no evidence he intends to heed the warning. He blames Romney for robbing him of his destiny; now he will return the curse. Like the demented Ahab, Gingrich seems intent on pursuing his quarry, even unto his own destruction, even unto the destruction of the Republican Party scow.

In other endorsement news, Jim DeMint, the state's junior senator, is playing coy with perhaps the most coveted endorsement in the GOP. Perhaps DeMint's blessing could save the party from its self-destructive spiral, but only if he gives it to Romney. It's inconceivable that the godfather of the Tea Party could ever support the "Massachusetts moderate."

And so we may be witnessing a tragedy of Shakespearean proportions. For a man of Newt Gingrich's grandiose ambitions and delusions to finally come to the end of his career, to witness his own downfall and debasement on the national stage, is perhaps more than his own jaded psyche can endure. We may be in for a great meltdown, a man personally and publicly humbled before the gods.

It's fitting that Newt should bring the penultimate act of his long, theatrical career to this little state, which still suffers from its own delusions of grandeur and which has never recovered from its own epic downfall. Newt Gingrich and South Carolina were made for each other.

January 18, 2012

(Gingrich did not air the "documentary" on Mitt Romney. He won the state GOP presidential primary on January 21, 2012, but faded soon after. He withdrew from the race in early May and endorsed Romney, who went on to win the nomination. It was the first time South Carolina Republicans failed to support the candidate who eventually became the party's presidential nominee.)

STATE OF IRONY
REPUBLICANS DESCEND ON SOUTH CAROLINA ON MLK DAY

Martin Luther King's birthday last week was a good time for reflection and remembrance. One of his favorite places in the world was Penn Center on St. Helena Island, in Beaufort County. The civil rights leader was fond of taking his lieutenants to the former Quaker school for a little R&R as they planned their historic campaign for social justice.

Last week's holiday was also a good time to take the racial temperature in South Carolina. While there has been little overt racism in the state in recent years, there is always potential violence bubbling just under the surface. It doesn't take much to bring it out.

It was with abundant irony that this little state with a Confederate flag on its Statehouse grounds, its generations of violent and blustery racism, and its dubious distinction of being the first to secede from the Union and the last to recognize the Martin Luther King holiday would become the center of the Republican universe for the two weeks around which we celebrate King's birthday.

The modern Republican Party — especially in the South — has never gotten comfortable with black people. Even as the GOP circus came to town, three of its leading presidential primary candidates were explaining or shrugging off racial gaffes they had recently made or that had recently come to light. And for the two weeks that they saturated the state with their TV ads and their presence, they played to overwhelmingly white audiences, audiences one suspects would have been rather hostile to the very idea of MLK Day. Indeed, during their numerous appearances in our state — individually and collectively — I heard only one passing reference to the birthday of one of the most important Americans of the twentieth century.

We got another glimpse at this awkward relationship — and at the cozy relationship between state agencies and employees and the GOP — when Dr. Walter Edgar interviewed state Sen. John

Courson on his weekly ETV Radio program the weekend before the primary. Dr. Edgar is the dean of South Carolina historians, the author of the most celebrated history of the state, and editor of *The South Carolina Encyclopedia.* He also cashes a state paycheck each month.

The subject of the interview was the rise of the Republican Party in South Carolina, from irrelevance 50 years ago to dominance today. And who better than Courson to tell the story? He is a 50-year GOP veteran, a three-time delegate to the Republican National Convention, and a 28-year member of the General Assembly.

For an hour Edgar quizzed Courson on the recent history of the state GOP, and for an hour Courson regaled him with personal memories and lessons in state political history. Among his recollections was the fact that he had been a Kennedy Democrat in 1960, but by 1964 he was a Goldwater Republican.

Why the switch? Courson didn't say and Edgar was too polite to ask. Edgar also neglected to point out that Courson was hardly the only person to switch parties in that critical four-year period. Strom Thurmond switched in the summer of 1964, as did a majority of white Southerners. In that year, the Palmetto State — like much of the South — voted for the GOP for the first time since Reconstruction, and the region has been overwhelmingly Republican ever since.

What could have caused such a sudden and seismic political shift? Edgar and Courson refused to bring up any unpleasantness, but history shows that during those critical four years the civil rights movement came into its own. It was embraced by Northern Democrats and a majority of the American people. Dr. King led his march to Washington and thrilled the nation with his transcendent words and presence. And in July 1964, a Democratic Congress passed and a Democratic president signed the Civil Rights Act, the most sweeping social reform since the end of slavery. White Southerners responded by leaving the Democratic Party and making the South a Republican stronghold.

That Dr. Edgar could conduct such an interview and not once

touch on this unsavory history is equivalent to talking for an hour about secession without once mentioning slavery. Many people have done this, of course, but they are not professional historians. The fact is that the same emotions that cause people to ignore slavery's role in secession also make it uncomfortable to discuss civil rights in connection to the rise of the GOP. But make no mistake, white Southerners seceded from the Union for essentially the same reason their great grandchildren seceded from the Democratic Party a century later.

That Walter Edgar did not ask Courson about the role of race in the rise of the Republican Party represents something close to malpractice. And he was aided and abetted by ETV Radio.

Happy Birthday, Dr. King.

January 25, 2012

FEAR & VOTING

"We have done our level best [to disenfranchise blacks] ...We stuffed ballot boxes. We shot them. We are not ashamed of it."

— *Sen. Benjamin R. Tillman, 1900*

THE STATE GOP STRIKES BACK
AFTER LOSSES, REPUBLICANS PLAN TO LIMIT VOTER ACCESS

Throughout most of its history, South Carolina has made the right to vote rare and precious. Before the Civil War, only white male property owners were granted suffrage. The state Constitution of 1895 established literacy tests and other barriers to keep blacks from the polls.

This was during the bad old days of white Democratic domination in the South. That came to an end with the Civil Rights Act of 1964 and the Voting Rights Act of 1965, passed by a Democratic Congress and signed by a Democratic president. Blacks registered to vote in unprecedented numbers across the South, and whites responded by bolting to the Republican Party. By 1972, the political face of the South had been transformed.

But some things never change. Yes, blacks vote and hold political office in greater numbers than ever before, and Republicans dominate Southern politics as surely as Democrats did a half-century ago. But white people are still trying to keep blacks from voting; they just use different methods to do it.

To be fair, this is not an exclusively Southern phenomenon. For some years the national Republican Party has been engaged in an insidious strategy to suppress the votes of minorities, students, the poor, and elderly around the nation.

Republican-majority legislatures in Georgia, Indiana, and other states have passed voter ID laws, ostensibly to protect the democratic process from voter fraud. What they have failed to do is show that there is any widespread or systematic voter fraud which would merit such a radical remedy.

In the week before last November's election, *The Nation* reported that in some states, "the Republican Party has made plans to challenge the legitimacy of thousands of voters using a notorious, legally dubious technique known as 'caging,' whereby the party sends out nonforwardable mail to low-income or minority households (the people likely to move frequently or be victims of subprime mortgage foreclosures) and uses returned envelopes to question the eligibility of the addressees."

Former S.C. House District 115 GOP Rep. Wallace Scarborough did something similar when he tried to overturn his defeat by Democrat Anne Peterson Hutto in November. Scarborough argued that people who received their mail some place other than their residence were committing voter fraud. The Charleston County Board of Elections and the S.C. Election Commission rejected his complaint, and Scarborough sought to have his House colleagues throw out the election, before finally abandoning the challenge.

According to *The Nation*, George W. Bush's Justice Department made a priority of going after alleged cases of individual voter fraud, while showing little interest in protecting the voting rights of minorities, as the Voting Rights Act mandates it to do. Indeed, the Bush Justice Department brought down a firestorm on its head by firing nine U.S. attorneys. It now appears that some of those attorneys were fired because they refused to pursue voter fraud cases when there was not enough evidence.

There is also strong reason to believe that the national Republican Party was laying the groundwork to claim massive voter fraud in the weeks leading up to the November election. The GOP and the right-wing media filled the airways and op-ed pages with bogus claims that ACORN, the national advocacy group for lower- and middle-class homeowners and workers, was involved in a vast campaign to fraudulently register voters.

If the presidential election had been close — or had turned on one or two key states — the Republicans would still be fighting to throw out votes and put John McCain in the White House. As it was, Barack Obama defeated McCain decisively in both the popular vote and Electoral College. Even Rush Limbaugh and Bill O'Reilly could not spin such a defeat into an ACORN conspiracy.

In South Carolina, Republicans were stunned last November when they lost two General Assembly seats and came surprisingly close to losing the 1st District congressional seat held by Henry Brown. These Democratic victories were the result of a huge black voter turnout, made possible, in part, by two weeks of absentee voting (also called early voting) prior to Election Day.

Now state Republicans are striking back with legislation designed to limit absentee voting and to require voters to have a photo ID. Of course, they are doing this in the name of preventing voter fraud, though no one has claimed any voter fraud in this state. What this legislation will actually do is limit voting access for the poor, elderly, and minorities. That is why the state branches of AARP, Common Cause, NAACP, the League of Women Voters, and ACLU are rallying to stop House Bill 3418 and Senate Bill 334.

April 1, 2009

(S.C. still has absentee voting. A very weakened version of voter ID became law in January 2013.)

STOP VOTER ID
THE REAL VOTER FRAUD IS GOING ON IN THE STATEHOUSE

It's as predictable as the first robin in spring. The General Assembly is in session, and Republicans are squealing like monkeys in a mango tree to pass some kind of voter ID bill.

We've been down this road before. It was a bad idea last year and the year before that and the year before that. And it looks like a good way to get the state embroiled in another big, hairy, no-win lawsuit, not to mention another segment on *The Daily Show*.

But damn the logic! Damn the expense! Republicans are moving ahead with reckless abandon. And they're serious this time! The 2008 election scared the hell out of them, thanks to a record black turnout, and they are not going to let that happen again.

What we are talking about here is a bill that would require registered voters to show a picture ID at the polling place before they are allowed to vote. And why would the Wise Ones in Columbia do such a thing?

Ask a GOPer and he will tell you that it's to prevent voter fraud — you know, where somebody pretends to be somebody he's not in order to vote. Ask him to show you an example of said voter fraud in South Carolina and he will give you the kind of deer-in-the-headlights stare that Sarah Palin gave Katie Couric when the CBS anchor asked the vice-presidential candidate what newspapers she read.

You see, there are no known cases of voter fraud in South Carolina in recent decades. And you could count all the cases of false-identity voter fraud in the whole country on your hands. Despite all the ranting and railing of the right-wing media, despite all the allegations and imputations against ACORN, no one has ever said that the community organizing group was trying to commit false-identity voter fraud. The worst thing they were found doing was getting false signatures on voter lists — names like Donald Duck and Minnie Mouse. I think these frauds would be stopped with or without a voter ID.

As Charleston attorney Armand Derfner told the *Statehouse Report* recently, "We've never had a complaint of that kind of fraud." The real fraud, he said, is this proposed law.

Not only is voter ID unnecessary; it's expensive. With our state's tax base shrinking, with teachers and other state employees being furloughed, with some of the worst schools in the nation and infrastructure years behind in maintenance, our General Assembly wants to spend over a million dollars to fund picture ID cards for thousands of people, provide training for poll workers, and pay for other expenses related to this ill-begotten piece of legislation.

Critics call this bill a solution in search of a problem — and a rather expensive solution at that. So again the question: Why?

The answer to that question is in the DNA of the GOP.

Voter ID is nothing less than a plan to disenfranchise 178,000 South Carolina voters. Yes, that's how many registered voters in this state have no picture ID, according to the State Elections Commission.

Republicans whine that it's no big deal. You need a picture ID to have a bank account or credit card, drive a car, get a passport — all the things that middle-class white people take for granted. And that's exactly the point. A lot of people in this historically poor state are not middle class. They don't have credit cards or bank accounts, cars or passports. But they do have the right to vote.

All of them are poor; most of them are black. And they are the very people that the white establishment has been trying to keep away from the polls for well over a century. In the past they have used literacy tests, grandfather laws, poll taxes, and other contrivances to preserve the social order. Voter ID follows in this same shameful tradition.

Because some people's resources — including transportation — are so limited, it could be an imposition to require them to go to the DMV to have their photo ID made. In a healthy democracy the legislature would do all in its power to expand the electorate. Our General Assembly has historically taken the opposite position.

Voter ID has passed the Senate and is working its way through the House. This stinker of a bill, H. 3418, will turn back the nearly half a century of progress this state has made in expanding the franchise. Don't let it happen.

Remember: The vote you save may be your own.

February 24, 2010

(A weakened version of voter ID went into effect in 2013.)

STEALING DEMOCRACY
S.C. REPUBLICANS DETERMINED TO DISENFRANCHISE BLACK VOTERS

Maybe it was idle curiosity. Maybe it was outright espionage. Whatever it was, it was perfectly legal.

Shortly after the 2008 election, Ann Beser and Steve Chand, of Myrtle Beach, saw the notice in the local paper that there would be a big breakfast confab of Republicans in Georgetown. Beser and Chand are not Republicans, but they are white, and that was good enough. So these two retirees drove down from Myrtle Beach to Georgetown to have grits and eggs with the GOPers.

Republicans at that meeting were in a surly mood. They had just lost the White House and the U.S. Senate. In South Carolina, Barack Obama had carried 45 percent of the popular vote — the most of any Democratic presidential candidate in decades — and inspired record black voter turnout.

Perhaps the moodiest of them all was Jill Kelso, who had lost the House District 108 race in Georgetown County to Vida Miller by a margin of 256 votes out of more than 17,000 cast. One of the GOPers addressing the room that day was Rep. Alan Clemmons, of Horry County, chair of the House Judiciary Committee. Clemmons denounced the "bus loads of voters" who came to the polls in Georgetown County the day before the election to cast absentee ballots, perhaps tipping the balance in Kelso's election and others.

Clemmons didn't have to say who was on those buses. To the great consternation of white politicians, black churches have been using those vehicles to get their people to the polls for generations. They call it "Souls to the Polls." But among certain whites, the phrase "bus loads of voters" — like "welfare queen" — has become code for black.

"We do not have early voting in this state," Clemmons declared, correctly enough. These bus loads of voters were abusing the system, he said, casting absentee ballots. Absentee voting is meant as a convenience for those who would not be able to vote on Election Day, he said. Beser got the clear message that Clemmons thought it was time for the General Assembly to do something about the bus loads of voters.

As eager as he was to fulminate about voting rights and wrongs in front of a room full of GOPers, Clemmons declined to return my call to discuss the issue for this column. Had he called back, I would have challenged him on his accusations: The bus loads of voters were perfectly within their rights to cast absentee ballots at the county voter registration office the day before the election. Perhaps they were going to be working on Election Day, or maybe they were going to be manning the polls at other sites and would not be able to cast votes in their home precincts.

That was the reason Beser and Chand cast absentee ballots in Myrtle Beach. And when they went to the voter registration office on the day before the election, they found the place packed with absentee voters. "People were obviously taking advantage of it, and it was obviously working," Beser told me.

Working too well, many Republicans believe. Their response — though it was three years in the making — is the controversial voter ID law. The League of Women Voters and the Associated Press have each studied the issue and concluded that close to 200,000 South Carolinians — mostly poor, mostly black — may be disenfranchised by this law. Our Republican governor and legislators still try to explain with perfectly straight faces that presenting a picture ID is the only way to deter voter fraud at the polls. What they cannot explain is where this voter fraud is taking place.

Chris Whitmire, a spokesman for the S.C. State Election Commission, told NPR two weeks ago that voter fraud has never been a problem. "We have no record of any confirmed case of that in South Carolina in recent history," he said.

So why the rush to fix a problem that doesn't exist? For the same reason that dozens of Republican state legislatures are doing it around the country. According to *Rolling Stone* magazine, a group called the American Legislative Exchange Council has provided GOP legislators with draft legislation based on Indiana's ID requirement: "In five states that passed such laws in the past year — Kansas, South Carolina, Tennessee, Texas, and Wisconsin —

the measures were sponsored by legislators who are members of ALEC."

What we are seeing in South Carolina is not isolated, nor is it an example of local whimsy. It is part of a coordinated, nationwide campaign by Republicans to take the vote from American citizens. It took the federal courts to throw out poll taxes and literacy tests in the 1960s. Let's hope they are up to the task of preserving democracy in the 21st century.

November 9, 2011

(A weakened version of voter ID went into effect in 2013.)

YOU LIE!
CALLING OUT REPUBLICANS ON VOTER ID

If you read South Carolina's daily newspapers, you can be forgiven if you have never heard of the American Legislative Exchange Council. ALEC is a corporate-funded juggernaut that works with Republicans in pushing a hard right-wing agenda, including anti-union legislation, the privatization of schools and prisons, and the rolling back of environmental regulations.

Another of ALEC's priorities is the passage of voter ID laws wherever possible. According to *In These Times* magazine, a total of 30 states already have such laws, which were unheard of five years ago. Eight others passed voter ID laws this year. South Carolina was among them.

Voter ID laws — wherever they are passed — have one thing in common. It is no longer enough to show a voter registration card to cast a ballot. Now one must show a photo ID, usually a driver's license.

Why the sudden compulsion to force voters to show their picture at the polls?

"The overall idea is pretty obvious," journalist Frances Fox

Piven told *In These Times*. "Both parties expect close elections in 2012, and if you can peel off just a couple of percentage points, you can determine the outcome."

Contrary to what Republicans would have you believe, voter ID has nothing to do with preserving the integrity of our elections. When was the last time a person was charged with impersonating another voter at the polls in South Carolina? It hasn't happened in at least 40 years, which is apparently how far the records go back on such matters. Nationwide, there have been fewer than two dozen cases in the past 20 years. Clearly there is no epidemic of voter fraud in this state or in the nation. So what exactly is the heart of the matter?

Most adults carry a driver's license with their picture on it. Those who don't are usually people who don't own cars or people who are too old to drive. In other words, poor people and others in need of social services. To put it more succinctly, people more likely to vote Democratic. This is what voter ID is really about — disenfranchising potential Democratic voters and peeling off those couple of percentage points on Election Day. There is no better evidence of this than the fact that many of the voter ID laws — including South Carolina's — do not accept a college student photo ID, even if it is issued by a state institution. Why no college student IDs? We got the answer in a video — which Stephen Colbert shared with the nation — of New Hampshire Republican House Speaker William O'Brien describing "liberal" students who must not be allowed to vote with their college ID cards. (The law passed the Republican legislature in the Granite State, but was vetoed by Democratic Gov. John Lynch.)

To those without driver's licenses, the Palmetto State's new voter ID law provides a special photo ID card, issued by the Department of Motor Vehicles. The estimated cost of issuing said ID cards to hundreds of thousands of people is a quarter-million dollars a year.

Of course, Republicans are betting it will not cost nearly so much. They're hoping that for the poor and elderly who don't have reliable transportation, just getting to the DMV will be such an imposition that they won't get an ID. The end result? They will just drop off the voter rolls and out of the electoral process. That is the two percent the Republicans are looking for.

And yet, as cynical as Republicans have shown themselves to be with their new voter ID law, they have actually trumped themselves with another bill, which Gov. Nikki Haley recently signed. The law allows military personnel to fax and e-mail their ballots from anywhere around the world and it eliminates a witness requirement for write-in ballots. As the *Post and Courier* points out, our GOP legislature seems quite unconcerned about fraud among this heavily Republican group of voters.

According to the S.C. League of Women Voters, close to 200,000 voters may be disenfranchised by the state's new voter ID law. And who are those voters? We got a glimpse into that community a couple of weeks ago with a *Post and Courier* story about area public transportation. There are 19,439 households without a car — and presumably, without a driver's license — in Charleston, North Charleston, and Summerville. Needless to say, they are overwhelmingly poor and black.

"These are our neighbors. These are people who live among us, who work beside us," S.C. ACLU Executive Director Victoria Middleton said. "Is that really what we want our General Assembly doing to our electoral system?"

Somebody thinks so. But don't be fooled. The next time a Republican tries to tell you that we need voter ID to protect the sanctity of the electoral process, just take a page from Rep. Joe Wilson's text, look the GOPer straight in the eye, and say, "You lie!"

August 31, 2011

(A weakened version of voter ID went into effect in 2013.)

THE WAR ON DEMOCRACY
HAVEN'T WE BEEN DOWN THIS ROAD BEFORE?

Was it coincidence or was it destiny? In this state, which is eternally reliving its past, the two seem indistinguishable.

On the day that state Attorney Gen. Alan Wilson swore to defend South Carolina's new voter ID law in federal court, the General Assembly was debating a new piece of legislation that would effectively shut down voter registration drives in the state.

The bill in question — H. 4549 — would stop voter registration drives by creating burdensome regulations and stiff penalties for violations, up to $1,000. Voter registration drives are as traditional as Fourth of July parades, and they have been organized for generations by the League of Women Voters, churches, and even Scouts trying to earn their citizenship badges.

But that will likely be a thing of the past if our GOP-controlled legislature prevails. The bill was pushed through the Judiciary Committee without even consulting the state Election Commission. The man doing the pushing was Rep. Alan Clemmons (R-Myrtle Beach), who is on record telling a band of GOPers after the 2008 election that the GOP would do whatever it could to keep Democrats from showing up in such threatening numbers in future elections.

The solution to all those Democrats on Election Day was the voter ID law, which requires voters to show a state-issued photo ID at the polls. The ostensible purpose of the law was to prevent voter fraud, but Republicans have not been able to present a case of voter fraud that would have been prevented by a photo ID. What we do know — and it is confirmed by the Election Commission and the League of Women Voters — is that the law could potentially disenfranchise nearly 200,000 mostly poor and rural (read: black) voters. It will also thin out college students and the elderly, all groups who have a stronger likelihood of voting Democratic.

The U.S. Justice Department immediately struck down the state voter ID law under the review provision of the 1965 Voting

Rights Act, and Wilson went to court to defend it. *The Post and Courier* has since reported that this bit of litigation is going to cost our cash-strapped state up to a million dollars. Now with the General Assembly moving ahead with another voter suppression law, it looks like we will see more litigation and more unnecessary expense.

H. 4549 does not address any recognized problem. The regulations and penalties imposed by the law have the ostensible purpose of keeping the registration process clean and open, but there have been no documented cases of people being improperly registered. The sole purpose of the law seems to be scaring people away from the civic goal of registering citizens to vote. Voter registration drives in schools, churches, and shopping malls are aimed at people who normally do not vote — and perhaps have never voted. Again, this profile tends to describe both young and minority demographics, two Democratic voting groups.

Something else the voter ID law has in common with this new voter-suppression bill is that both came out of the American Legislative Exchange Council, a right-wing, pro-business organization created to bring Republican state legislators and business leaders together to promote their mutual interests. ALEC has championed laws supporting private education vouchers and curtailing the power of unions. One of the biggest goals ALEC has worked on is having states pass harsher sentencing laws with the purpose of putting more people in jail for longer periods. This is done at the behest of the private prison industry, a big ALEC supporter. And of course, another goal has been to get Democratic voters off the voter rolls, assuring Republican victories in state and federal elections. Florida has already passed this piece of ALEC-sponsored legislation. Now it's South Carolina's turn.

The tragedy, of course, is not just with this fraudulent bill and the fraudulent men and women who want to pass it. The tragedy is that this is just the latest example of our state waging war on itself. The history of this little state is the story of the dominant group trying to punish, deprive, and exclude all others. Whether it's Jim Crow laws, the exclusion of women from the Citadel, the denial of full rights to gays and lesbians, or trumped-up laws to disenfranchise voters, it is a story that has been going on for generations. Other states take measures to punish their minorities, of course, but probably none does it more frequently, more sweepingly than South Carolina. It is this self-loathing and self-destruction that has put this state in a nineteenth century downward spiral, that makes us look abhorrent and intolerant to the world, that holds us back economically and socially, and that ultimately poisons our souls.

February 15, 2012

(H.4549 did not become law.)

DOWNWITHTILLMAN.COM